FROM OUR FALL

The Separation Anxiety We Experience
and Unified Peace We Can Achieve

Jacob Pannell

WESTBOW
PRESS®
A DIVISION OF THOMAS NELSON
& ZONDERVAN

This book is a work of non-fiction. Unless otherwise noted, the author and the publisher make no explicit guarantees as to the accuracy of the information contained in this book and in some cases, names of people and places have been altered to protect their privacy.

Scripture quotations are from the ESV® Bible (The Holy Bible, English Standard Version®), copyright © 2001 by Crossway, a publishing ministry of Good News Publishers. Used by permission. All rights reserved.

WestBow Press books may be ordered through booksellers or by contacting:

WestBow Press
A Division of Thomas Nelson & Zondervan
1663 Liberty Drive
Bloomington, IN 47403
www.westbowpress.com
1 (866) 928-1240

Because of the dynamic nature of the Internet, any web addresses or links contained in this book may have changed since publication and may no longer be valid. The views expressed in this work are solely those of the author and do not necessarily reflect the views of the publisher, and the publisher hereby disclaims any responsibility for them.

Any people depicted in stock imagery provided by Getty Images are models, and such images are being used for illustrative purposes only. Certain stock imagery © Getty Images.

ISBN: 978-1-9736-4498-9 (sc)
ISBN: 978-1-9736-4497-2 (hc)
ISBN: 978-1-9736-4499-6 (e)

Library of Congress Control Number: 2018913433

Print information available on the last page.

WestBow Press rev. date: 12/04/2018

CONTENTS

ACKNOWLEDGEMENTS

Thank you to my wife, Lindsey. This book
would be impossible without you.

Thank you to Ken Martin who raised this book to
readability through his editing prowess.

I would not be here without you – the nameless many who found the strength to share their faith with my forefathers who found the strength to share their faith with me. So, I pass it on to you. How I wish to meet you in person so that our faith may grow together. For many who read this, we will not commune until we pass from this life. Yet, I feel remiss because perhaps our faith together could move mountains. Perhaps that is the true secret-that in communion, we could find the mustard-seed faith to move mountains. Perhaps, though, my tiny little faith may add to yours and you will be the one to truly move mountains, and so I lend you my faith. I have often heard as men grow older they find themselves disagreeing with what they wrote in their youth. I hope these words stand the test of time. My hope is to give you the truth.

You must know up front that these ideas are not coming from a well-educated theologian. I do not hold any advanced training in any seminary, though I would find that training useful and fascinating. Yet, I do not count that as a loss. This only enables God to work all the more in that weakness. Thus, it is important to note that anything stolen or lifted from other works is not intentional. If I have plagiarized you in any way, I would love to credit your work, as it will only give further credit to the arguments. Beyond that, it will be easy for you to know what is from God and what is from my human weakness. I have not been trained in all of the theological arguments and their pros and cons. Where I stand is the understanding that God has afforded me from my study of the Bible. So, if you learn something or God is revealed in a new and special way, you can be sure it was His doing and not mine. If there is any weakness, you can be sure it is mine and not God's. Please afford my weaknesses the Grace that God has given you, and hopefully you will grow closer to him while reading this work.

INTRODUCTION

This is a book about relationships. I believe that everyone can have satisfying relationships, regardless of age, race, sex, nationality, or another identifier. I believe that everyone can come to know a God who is actively attempting to engage them. I believe that it is through the relationships that we will explore in this book that we can encounter, come to know and grow closer with this God becoming like Jesus Christ. I believe that as Christians our lives revolve around gospel-centered discipleship. This is achieved by knowing, experiencing, and worshipping God, Jesus and the Holy Spirit. A person knows, experiences and worships God in both private and in community. Both the private relationship and communal relationship are indispensable for a satisfying relationship with God.

I want to engage you as a member of the community of Christ in a gospel-centered manner. I am doing this by writing to deepen your and my relationship with God, so that we may be satisfied together. However, unless you see me regularly in person, this satisfaction will be difficult to achieve. We must both be intertwined in the communities of faith in the location God has placed us. Full satisfaction may not be achieved during our lifetime.

This writing deepens our relationship with God by attempting to answer two questions: 1. Why is the world the way it is? 2. What can be done about it? This book is divided into two parts-one for each question. Both parts are necessary to understand fully any idea that I put forth.

I begin to answer these questions by looking back at some of our earliest recorded history, the Genesis 3 Fall of Humanity. In this story we can find some foundation for what's going on today. In a lot of ways, it is ugly, but it is who we are. I have come to understand four fundamental breaks or separations that we all encounter. I believe we have been separated from each other, nature, our own selves, and God. Much of our anxiety today can be traced back to these four separations.

It is not all ugly though. We have incredible potential to connect. We do not need to live in the anxiety created by these separations because we do not need to be separated. We can find a beautiful peace reached through unity. The second part of this book will look into the peaceful unity that lies within in our grasp.

Some concepts and ideas are difficult, and you will probably not agree with them at first blush. I encourage you not to judge this book on the first half, but rather the complete work. The brokenness, the problem, and the common human experience is in the first half. Discovering who we are has a certain beauty, and it will only get better as hope will arrive in the second part of the book. Ideas will be completed in the second part; so, if you feel wanting in the first half, keep going (it is kind of on purpose to leave you wanting a little). In the end, thank you for reading this. I hope it encourages your faith because writing it has encouraged mine.

PART 1

CHAPTER 1

SEPARATION ANXIETY

One of the most pertinent questions facing us today is, "why are we lonely?" We live in a more connected world than ever before. Social media allows me, an American, to connect with Malaysians, Arabs, and Germans whom I will likely never meet. Our interactions are scaled to new heights. We interact with not a few people but a few hundred or thousand every day, maybe even every hour. With all that interaction, we are still lonely. It is because all that interaction actually raises our awareness of how separated and therefore how lonely we truly are.

Our brains, whether we realize it or not, are aware of this separation and loneliness generated from the façade of the internet. Our increased loneliness develops an increased anxiety. The average person under 35 has the same anxiety level as a person hospitalized for anxiety in the 1950s.[1] Let that sink in. By the standards set in the 1950s, about 25% of the total U.S. population would be considered mental health patients. Anxiety due to our separation is our reality now more than ever.

I believe separation anxiety explains many of the problems in our world. Separation anxiety is a loaded phrase, so we are going to have to break it down and redefine its pieces so we can rebuild it into something to which everything can relate. When I speak of separation anxiety, I am not referring to the psychological diagnosis. I reach to something deeper, within all of us, regardless of our psychological states.

Take a moment and examine the difficult times of your life. I imagine that, almost always, those trials root in a misunderstanding or lack of connection and community. Much of the human experience can be summed up in attempts to generate genuine connections with others, so we belong. We desire to be a part of something, but we often fail. Our failure to connect creates anxiety. The failure to connect creates anxieties that drive our daily actions and the long arc of our lives. The world is a result of anxiety created by separation. We need to understand how separation anxiety occurs and the extent of its impact to understand why we are where we are today. Once we understand our separation anxiety, we can ask and answer, "What can we do about it?"

To begin, we need to define separation:

The action or state of moving or being moved apart.[2]

This definition implies we were once together. To be moved apart, we had to be together at one point. It will be helpful to ask a few questions. When was that time of togetherness? What exactly occurred to cause the separation? From what are we even separated?

BEFORE THE SEPARATION

"Adam and his wife were both naked, and they felt no shame."
Genesis 2:25[3]

I believe this is the moment of true togetherness. We felt no shame toward anything. We were naked before one another, nature, and God. "Shame" and "naked" are two key words in this verse. "Shame" denotes impending separation. The word "naked" describes the completeness or fullness of exposure and a union reaches beyond what is being worn. "Naked" relates to a peace achieved due to complete exposure, a *shalom* which we will talk about more later. Dietrich Bonhoeffer, in his work *Ethics,* defines "shame" as disunion. Disunion is created by the realization of a lack of something. Adam and Eve had no disunity at this point because there was no shame. They lacked nothing from each other or for each other. They lacked nothing from nature or from God. They were their truest and most open selves, naked before all the world had to offer.

2

Can you imagine a point in your life when you felt no shame? This would mean you felt no inferiority or superiority in anything. You were naked, perhaps, before a lover, and you enjoyed that person as much as he or she enjoyed you. Usually, however, at least one person feels inferior, feels shame, cockiness and/or superiority. Thus, nakedness is a difficult position to find. We can find it, but the search is not without effort. In the case of the lover, men may lead women in the path, but the woman must decide to follow. It is a delicate dance, where the initial burden of responsibility lies with men and ends with women. A dance requires two, so they must keep the beat together, or intimacy cannot be achieved.

Initially, Adam and Eve lived a life of no shame. They were partners in the truest sense. I am fortunate enough to catch glimpses of their paradise in my own marriage. When I listen to my wife, she is cleansed her of any shame, and when I reveal my own deficiencies, so she can cleanse me. But Adam and Eve's lack of shame did not last. What happened? I believe they became anxious. They lacked faith in one another and in God.

> Anxiety - a feeling of worry, nervousness, or unease, typically about an imminent event or something with an uncertain outcome.[4]

Ultimately, what became of them was uncertainty, which is the root of anxiety and the opposite of faith. They became uncertain of themselves, then each other, then nature, and finally God. They were anxious about finding the beat in the cacophony of sound. They became unsure of love. Would love really hold them together forever? Could they really trust each other and God?

THE FALL

> "When the woman saw that the fruit of the tree was good for food and pleasing to the eye, and also desirable for gaining wisdom, she took some and ate it. She also gave some to her husband, who was with her, and he ate it.[7] Then the eyes of both of them were opened, and they

realized they were naked; so, they sewed fig leaves together and made coverings for themselves."

Genesis 3:6 –7

Eve lost faith for a moment just long enough to let anxiety settle in and to let fear grip her. Women, do you feel the remnants today? Do you wake in the middle of the night anxious about your children, husband, or career? Not sensing the folly and only observing the upsides, Eve took the fruit and sought to end her anxiety on her own by gaining knowledge, certainty. In reality, the fruit brought separation with it.

Do not think I belittle the part Adam plays (or does not play) in this story. I do not wish to demean my sisters. Eve's protector and partner was with her while this tragedy occurred. Her strength, Adam, failed her. He was as much responsible for this fall as she was. Adam was surely one with the earth; he was made from it. Eve's connection is drawn through Adam. He knew what was happening. He did not support her or fight for her. Adam left Eve to wallow in anxiety. Eve was Adam's responsibility because she was made from his flesh. He failed her as she ate, and then, due to his own anxiety and shame, he ate as well. While originally complete in unity, Adam and Eve chose knowledge over faith, which led to choosing separation over love.

CONSEQUENCES OF THE FALL

"Then the eyes of both of them were opened, and they realized they were naked; so, they sewed fig leaves together and made coverings for themselves. Then the man and his wife heard the sound of the LORD God as he was walking in the garden in the cool of the day, and they hid from the LORD God among the trees of the garden.

> The man said, "The woman you put here with me—she gave me some
>   fruit from the tree, and I ate it."
> To the woman he said,
> "I will make your pains in childbearing very severe;
>   with painful labor you will give birth to children.

Your desire will be for your husband,
    and he will rule over you."

To Adam he said, "Because you listened to your wife and ate fruit from
    the tree about which I commanded you, 'You must not eat from it,'
"Cursed is the ground because of you;
    through painful toil you will eat food from it
    all the days of your life.
It will produce thorns and thistles for you,
    and you will eat the plants of the field.
By the sweat of your brow
    you will eat your food
until you return to the ground,
    since from it you were taken;
for dust you are
    and to dust you will return."

Genesis 3:7-8, 12, 16-19

This passage of scripture lists the curses that came into the world as a result of Adam and Eve eating of the Tree of the Knowledge of Good and Evil. These six verses reveal four fundamental separations that occur in our lives and cause us to be anxious. The separations are the separation of human from human, separation of human from nature, separation of human from his/her own self, and separation of human from God. Realize that God did not curse Adam and Eve with all these separations. Rather, the pronouncement from God is meant to reveal the separations that have already occurred by their eating of the Tree of the Knowledge of Good and Evil. It is imperative that we begin to understand these separations were not a choice made by God but a trade made by us. The trade was peace, unity, and faith for knowledge and a false sense of certainty that brings separation and anxiety.

Evidence for the separation that now occurs between human beings begins to show itself in verse 7. As we recognize our own failures, we focus on the failures of others. In verse 12, Adam shifts the blame from himself to Eve. He successfully lengthens the growing chasm between them by shoving her under the proverbial bus before God. He does not even stand

5

up for her. Adam, foolishly, tries to sever ties with Eve, even though she is "flesh of his flesh and bone of his bones." It is foolish to cut away someone who is part of your soul.

Adam, then, tries to blame God for the problem in verse 12 by saying, "The woman you placed here." Adam did nothing for Eve as she ate. Now, he does not want her anymore, even though she was quite literally made for him. Adam displays the fundamental weakness of man in this conversation, and I am no different without the Holy Spirit.

Still, Eve and womankind bear much of the weight in this separation. God placed man over woman, so now she can only fulfill her role of helpmate now, and be ruled over. God identifies who will be the future leader of the family. Before, it was a true partnership. Now, Adam must hold final responsibility. Before, Eve was held accountable for her own actions. Now, Adam must see to her needs and she to his, just as a medieval lord must follow the social contract between his people. This contract can either be abused or upheld. History is filled with men and women who trashed this contract and others who fought for it.

The separation continues with nature in verses 17-19. Adam is particularly cursed. Though he was made of earth and had power to control it, he can no longer use this ability to feed himself. Now, he must work the ground as we do today. Adam will now be subject to the harshness of nature. Dominion over nature will now only come with enforced respect and subjugation.

Next, the evidence for man's separation from himself is seen in verse 7. I imagine that moment as Adam and Eve looked at each other and realized they were naked. This is not the awkward part, for they were made for each other. They still delight in one another, but that feeling of inferiority creeps in, and they feel ashamed of themselves. Adam realizes that he was not strong enough to save his partner, Eve. Eve finds that she led her love, Adam, down an unchangeable path. They are disgusted with themselves. Adam cannot believe he failed Eve. Eve cannot believe she failed Adam. They have realized their internal disfunction, and so they have shame. They quickly work to cover the guilt and the fault they find within themselves by wearing fig leaves. The shame begins internally and ends externally as they cover their bodies to hide their souls.

Finally, and perhaps most significantly, Adam and Eve are separated from God. In verse 8 they hide from Him[5]. They attempt to hide from an omnipotent, omniscient and omnipresent God. Do we try to hide from the being that holds our molecules together? We know our evil as Adam and Eve did, and we hide. We choose to abandon a united relationship for knowledge because of our lack of trust in the goodness of the Lord Almighty.

THE ANXIETIES

From our four separations, we draw anxieties. We are anxious with our fellow man, with nature, with even ourselves, and with God. This anxiety is often felt as a basic distrust. I rarely trust my fellow man. Do you trust nature to provide? I do not. I have a stocked refrigerator and pantry just because I do not believe nature will provide. I do not even trust myself since I can overreact or waste time consuming instead of engaging my family or others. Worse still, I lie to myself about how great I am. I do not think I am alone in these feelings. Everyone has these moments where they let themselves down. It is so odd to think about failing yourself. This ought to be impossible, but there is separation in with us and so we experience anxiety in our own selves. All of this is driven by the deeper mistrust of the Lord God Almighty. We do not believe in him. We do not trust his power. Adam and Eve's actions in the Garden of Eden demonstrate our inability to trust God from the beginning of time.

How can we apply these thousands-of-years-old problems to today? To answer that question, we must understand anxiety. We can explore the separation anxiety by asking three questions: How do we succumb to, ignore, and overcome anxiety? We can then apply knowledge to our unique anxiety surrounding the four separations. This is not a new phenomenon. We are linked back thousands of generations through the same emotions and experiences regarding our separation anxiety. This link allows us to learn from them and do something practical to change.

HOW DO WE SUCCUMB TO ANXIETY?

The question of how we succumb to anxiety is related to our experience of severed connections. The separations (fellow human, nature, self, and

God) do not necessarily indicate immediate anxiety. We can overcome or ignore much of the anxiety surrounding us, even from birth. Succumbing to separation anxiety is rooted in the upfront reality that we are isolated at a fundamental level.

Anxiety comes when we are faced with the reality of isolation. Succumbing to this anxiety is when we cannot move through or past this reality to live out our normal life. Remaining in this anxiety will subtly change our entire life to incorporate the severed connection. Perhaps the most common way we can understand an anxiety reaction is through the emotion of fear.

It is the fear of severed connection that plagues us. Phobias are an extreme illustration of this point. Almost any phobia can be tied to the feared repetition of a negative experience. This negative experience is a broken trust. When our trust is broken, our fears can drive us to act irrationally. Irrationality extends beyond the object of the severed connection.

Let me provide an example concerning arachnophobia, the fear of spiders. It is a quite common and biologically necessary fear. The phobia, however, often grows with every interaction because the connection has been broken between a person and spiders, or the object of the fear. Continual positive experiences can re-establish the connection, but the initial negative experience and any other negative interactions only distance us further.

To dive in to the example, imagine you were bitten by a spider when you were five years old, eight years old, and again when you were 12 years old. This would cause natural arachnophobia, despite a number of possible positive experiences, because you will view spiders through the lens of pain in the initial experiences. Over time, your fear might become paralyzing, despite a potential deeper understanding of the necessity of spiders.

Arachnophobia, in this case, ultimately demonstrates our emotions resulting from separations dictate our responses to the impending anxiety. In the case of succumbing to anxiety, fear is a relatable major emotion, and we can see how we succumb to any number of separations, small or large.

Emotions drive our decisions when we are faced with separation anxiety, whether we succumb to, ignore, or overcome it. In the example, we saw the emotion above the fear, and that emotion persisted in our succumbing to the anxiety about spiders. We will continue to explore the emotions tied to the other ways of dealing with anxiety, ignoring or overcoming.

HOW DO WE IGNORE ANXIETY?

Succumbing to anxiety is not our only option. We may all experience the fear of succumbing to our anxiety. Far more common today is ignoring anxiety. After all, we do not have time to work through problems. We have lives to live and things to do, like Netflix queues. Those shows are not going to watch themselves! The most common emotion I have found behind ignoring anxiety is shame. Recall that shame is the realization that you are lacking something. Perhaps you lack skills, time, or other resources to work through an anxiety. We do not wish to succumb to the anxiety, so we simply ignore it. While succumbing to anxiety is experiencing a severed connection repeatedly, ignoring anxiety is not experiencing anything by choice.

The result is a person, we can call him Bob, who generally, cannot process emotions by choice. Bob lives a cold and calculating lifestyle, taking no joy nor heartache from life. Bob sees the separations, and he chooses to neither connect nor disconnect. Oftentimes, Bob works for the good of his fellow man, so his compatriot can enjoy better connections. Bob knows everyone without ever actually being known himself. Hopefully this leads Bob to have compassion on his fellow man. The other side, in Bob's pursuit of the common good, he loses perspective on what the common good actually means. In the end, Bob may only work for his own well-being, though he started by working for everyone.

In the end, anxiety catches up with us. We can ignore heartache and pain only for so long while not experiencing joy. Certainly, someone may do it for decades or even a lifetime, but most cannot. Humans are wired for emotion. For most of us, we will eventually succumb to anxiety or learn to overcome it.

HOW DO WE OVERCOME ANXIETY?

Vulnerability is the emotion behind overcoming anxiety. We are wise to reach out, to fight, and to make connections by being vulnerable. This is incredibly difficult for most of us, but the results are in 50 years of marriage, life-long friendships, and general happiness and joy. As Brené Brown, a researcher storyteller, said, "If we are going to find our way back to each other, vulnerability is going to be that path."[6] The published results of a 75-year studied concluded that strong and secure relationship were the key to longevity and happiness of people, regardless of social status or class.[7]

Dr. Brown defines vulnerability as "emotional risk, exposure, uncertainty." We can do vulnerability. We must do vulnerability all the time. We expose our weak human frame to the world out there, and we get burned. The burn creates anxiety for the next time we become vulnerable, to other people, nature, ourselves, or to God. Those who choose to expose themselves again and again experience the benefits of overcoming anxiety.

DIVING IN

So, we now have a way to examine the anxieties that have beset us during and since the Genesis 3 account. Armed with questions about the emotions behind how we succumb to, ignore, and overcome anxieties we can dig in and try to perceive how they affect us today. The goal is to understand how to create unique solution for your own life and situation. I want you to be able to take small risks, small vulnerabilities and reach a lasting peace. Example solutions will be explored in the second part of the book.

For now, though, we can dive into the separations occurring in our lives and in the lives of our ancestors. I hope you will be able to imagine some instances in your own life demonstrating the separations and the anxieties. I mean no harm or judgment for anyone reading through these separation anxieties. All of these are examples from history, near and far. Each chapter is incomplete without reading its counterpart in the second part of the book. I urge you not to judge one section on its own, but to measure it by the book as a whole. Each example has a purpose in demonstrating the major themes of the book where are we, how did we get here, and what can we do about it?

CHAPTER 2

SEPARATION AMONG PEOPLE

He said to them, "Because of your hardness of heart Moses
allowed you to divorce your wives, but from the beginning
it was not so."

Matthew 19:8

The separation of man from man might be the most apparent of the
four separations. I feel it every day. I walk down the street and accidently
bump into someone and it ruins their day. Someone cuts me off in traffic,
and I rage with anger. I could commit a crime and ruin a life. Our separation
from man encompasses all of our interactions with other humans.

But what is driving the separation between people? The knowledge
of good and evil is the basis for this separation. When Adam and Eve
ate the fruit, they did so with purpose. They sought the right to discern
good and evil. The serpent in the story saw their desire to judge what is
moral and immoral and twisted it within them. I picture the cunning
serpent convincing Eve that eating the fruit would actually give her a closer
relationship to her husband, God, or both. In reality, she and Adam gained
differing points of view. They gained the knowledge of the continuum of
good and evil exist, not necessarily the fixed definition of God.

Bonhoeffer notes in *Ethics* that having the knowledge of good and evil
gives us the ability to judge both good and evil. Take that in. At one point,
we did not know the difference between good and evil. All separations

between us come from differences of opinion affecting us in the past, present, and future. When we look to the past, we can see or know what is good and evil, but we cannot know the future, and so, we judge improperly what is good and evil in the present. Our knowledge gives us a false sense of understanding about good and evil, so we frequently misjudge based on the limited knowledge we have of the moment. We have to make these judgements on good and evil in a moment of incomplete understanding. God did not intend for us to make this judgement. We chose to have these differences of opinion over having the will of God. Let's look into an example of the difficulty of good and evil in the moment.

Before the Fall, we were united in singular purpose: to bring about good for the glory of God by doing His will. Having knowledge of good and evil put us into different perspectives on what is good and what is evil. An example may shed some light. In the 1940s in the United States, it was good to watch your neighbors from Asia, particularly those with Japanese ancestry. Many Japanese descendants were placed into internment camps, not wholly dissimilar to those in Nazi Germany. As a "good" American you would turn in any "suspicious activity" from your Japanese neighbor. This action was viewed as good from the point of view of the United States. However, for the citizens who were wrongfully imprisoned, it was an act of evil. Knowledge and perspective from multiple points of view are needed to understand good and evil, which has changed throughout history based on perspective. Our separation from other people is centered around the questions of what is good and what is evil? Those questions are what drive our separation.

The will of God is what united us before the Fall. Adam and Eve sought to do it. The would each have a place of importance and honor. Adam and Eve were each striving to do the will of God. Now, since the Fall, we strive for what we view as good in the moment, doing the best we can.

SUCCUMBING TO THE ANXIETY WITH OTHER PEOPLE

I do not want you to take for granted what this curse, – the separation from other people, – holds. You need to look no further than Genesis 4 to understand this concept. The story of Cain and Abel outlines the struggle of the knowledge of good and evil. Instead of doing God's will, Cain does what he thinks is "good." His brother Abel does the will of God, which is what is actually good. God blesses Abel for doing God's will, and Cain gets jealous, determining his brother is evil, and he kills him. Why does Cain find Abel evil? Cain finds Abel evil because there are severed connections. Abel is perceived by Cain to have a stronger attachment to God, while Cain's attachment has been weakened in his own eyes. Abel appears to have risen above Cain. Abel's blessings generate a severed connection between the brothers. From these severed relationships, Cain now feels anger, which only hides his fear. He fears any number of things such as his own weakness, he is not loved as much as Abel by God or by his parents, his brother will always outdo him, or Abel will become his master. The point is that fear from severed connections generates negativity, which will change our views. In this case, it is Cain's view of Abel. Cain believes Abel is evil, and in confronting him, he kills Abel.

The knowledge of good and evil has provided something for us. We can no longer be certain of another person's intentions. We feel fear toward and from other people. When we succumb to the anxiety induced by our separation from other people, we act out of fear in two basic ways: aggression or regression.

The most visible way of acting out of fear is aggression. Aggression, in our society, has very limited confines. Those who act aggressively out of those confines are disparaged. Perhaps, a comic book villain, such as Dr. Doom or the Joker can give us good examples of an aggressive person, but they are not real. They are over-dramatized versions of what we encounter every day. The bully at school or at work is far more real. Perhaps for you, it is the person who steps on people on their way up the corporate ladder. We can all think of someone who is the villain in our life. That person is often overly aggressive toward you. Imagine, though, how you might be another person's villain. All of us can act aggressively out of our own fears. When we act aggressively, we are succumbing to our separation anxiety.

The other way to act out of fear is regressing. Instead of overreacting, as the aggressor does, we underreact and withdraw. We allow the bully to push us around, or we do not depend on others because we are afraid they will let us down. Our fears lead us to live separated lives by being withdrawn.

In the end, both aggression and regression push people away. One attacks and the other retreats. Let us look at a historical example of succumbing to separation anxiety. The ancient Spartan civilization is known for achieving military and human perfection. It was, however, achieved at great cost. A "good" woman of Sparta civilized state would inspect her newborn child at a ritual site near the edge of a cliff. If the newborn did not pass inspection, then she would promptly toss the newborn off of the cliff. The "evil" woman would fight for her child or hide the child from inspection. The women found avoiding the ritual would be cast from society. This civilization has been scorned for nearly a millennium for the number of children lost and women murdered in the pursuit of human perfection. Imagine the fear reigning in that society. Being cast out of your society was a death sentence, so you murdered your child, or you left to fend for yourself. Some women believed in the Spartan way, and it was no trouble to toss an imperfect child over the cliff. The price for the knowledge of good and evil was so steep mothers willingly threw their children to their deaths and were thought of as "good" parents!

IGNORE THE ANXIETY CREATED AMONG OUR FELLOW PERSONS

Beyond aggression or withdrawal, we can also choose to ignore each other. The angst felt by those who succumb to anxiety is usually provided by external stimuli, and ignoring anxiety is felt from within. Remember, the emotion attached to ignorance is shame. Shame is the realization of our own lacking. Because of our own deficiencies, we hide and ignore the external anxiety. While this method may prove peaceful, we do not take the time to know anyone. Every relationship is kept at a surface level. There is neither aggression nor regression. Engagement is required to reach a state of fear. While this apathy might seem like a viable solution to disconnection, it is not. Atrocities are committed by the uncaring, often for the sake of convenience. The growth and health of society as a whole are neither here nor there in the individual's mind because he or she never takes responsibility for anyone's actions but his or her own. All of our actions are carefully calculated and justified in our minds, but in the end, we are not the judge.

A good example of uncaring is found in the United States, though it was not constructed on this principle. It began as a nation founded on care for others. One of its most famous monuments, the Statue of Liberty, reads:

"Give me your tired, your poor,
Your huddled masses, yearning to breathe free,
The wretched refuse of your teeming shore,
Send these, the homeless, tempest tost to me,
I lift my lamp beside the golden door."

Yet, about a million new lives are terminated every year in a legalized manner. The apathy of the United States appears even worse than that of the Spartans. We kill our newborns in the womb. The Spartans at least waited to see if their children could amount to physical perfection. We kill them before we even have a chance to know them. Over the last 40 years, more than 43 million unborn lives have been lost according to the Centers for Disease Control.[8]

This number is so vast, we need some perspective. Adolf Hitler, one of the most famous mass murderers of history, was only able to kill about six million Jews in five years. Almost the same number of abortions occurred between 1996-2000. Furthermore, Hitler would have long run out of populace to kill had he reached 43 million. Yet someone was far better than Hitler at sanctioning mass murder. Joseph Stalin has an estimated 30 million deaths to his count over 30 years. That puts Stalin at 10 million a decade. These men were trying to kill the maximum number of people they could as fast as they could. Yet neither matches the abortion rate in the United States. At nearly 33 percent more deaths than Stalin, the United States has effectively and efficiently killed their populace before they were even born.

An interesting thought is about those who would take in the wretched refuse of the world will not even allow their own children to be born. The sad thing is we have sanctioned this because it protects those already alive. It protects the women who would choose this procedure because they have been mistreated. The sanctioning of abortion is not about the children. It is about the country-wide mistreatment of women. The women who chose this procedure are not protected and cared for. The many of the powerful in this country do not care to protect the women, only shame them. Simply refer to the #MeToo and subsequent #ChurchToo movements.

Abortion highlights the separation between man and woman, not just mother and child. The men of this country do not protect their women and so women choose the only option, to take care of themselves. Men do not offer women safety and protection because we are incapable of taking the responsibility assigned to us in the fall, headship. It is our role to lead which means it is our role to protect and support women. Even the Bible tells us woman is the glory of man.[9] If this is true we are not a very glorious people. Abortion is certainly a mother and child issue, but it is a larger indicator of how we, men, treat, think about and respect women.

When we ignore the anxiety created between people, death follows. Ignorance on this scale is unacceptable. We kill the next Albert Einstein, Niels Bohr, Pablo Picasso, Robert Frost, Socrates, and General George Patton without even letting them take a breath. The anxiety of our separation hits us just as deeply as it hits our ancient ancestors. It has not changed from the first biblical family until now.[10] Killing our emotions is not the answer. We have to react healthily toward them.

OVERCOMING ANXIETY BETWEEN MEN

The separation between people takes on a different emotion when we overcome the anxiety, vulnerability. Vulnerability is a risk because sometimes the other person with whom you are vulnerable can end up knowing you better than you do. This gives the person power over you, which can leave you exposed to his or her attacks. You might never recover from the hurt and, thus, succumb to the anxiety, or you might avoid the hurt altogether and simply have apathy for the separation.

What differentiates the overcomer is the person with whom you are vulnerable is a choice. You are in control. You choose to open up to the other person. It may be a select few or even just one. It is difficult to be vulnerable with more than a tiny group. Even Jesus had an inner circle of three. I cannot imagine having more than a the few, except with the possible addition of a spouse. But, how does vulnerability with a few function? While there are a few examples of this type of relationship outside the confines of marriage, David and Jonathan in 1 Samuel for example, marriage is something with which we are more familiar. We can look at some of the traits of marriage to learn how to apply them safely outside of marriage.

Marriage is the continual choice to be open and vulnerable with one person until death parts you. I agree with the Apostle Paul when he says it is a "great mystery," because the only way to really know that relational vulnerability is to be married. The institution is so interesting to me because it is one of the few links existing before the Fall. Because it existed pre-fall, we can learn something from the original union and apply it to the broader experience.

The original marriage was meant to be a full partnership. As the younger spouse, Eve would have to look to Adam in times of need. Though Adam brought wisdom to the relationship, Eve brought vitality and connection. Adam needed Eve's traits just as much as Eve needed his wisdom and strength. They co-habitated and built a vulnerable relationship with one another. Think of your partner knowing everything about you. Your partner fully comprehends all of your faults and works to cover them with their own strengths. You, in turn, do the same. You understand your partner's faults and work to cover them with your strengths. In this partnership, vulnerability means getting the job done better. What is the job? It is working from the singular perspective to do what God has provided for the two partners. God gave the earth to Adam to subdue and gave Eve as his helper in that task. By being open and vulnerable, Adam and Eve could accomplish the task set before them.

The first marriage sometimes sounds so different from the present. Today my wife does not know me as well as Eve knew Adam. I do not know her as well as Adam knew Eve. We are separated, despite our intense longing to become one. She does not have the scars or victories that I do. Even if I could share everything, I probably would not. I hide my shame. I choose separation because I fear she would rather be separated than ashamed of me. Because of my fear and shame, we do not accomplish all of the things God has set before us. For example, one of the constant pressure points for us is how to parent our children. As the parent who stays at home, I have a lot of information on how our child might react in a certain situation. She feels that it is her role, though, to be the primary parent in those same situations. I do not disagree with her feelings, but it does not always lead to us accomplishing the task in the best manner. She tries to lead in parenting, and I am too passive when I need to step in. In this example, I am ashamed to be the stay-at-home parent because I feel like I should be the one with a job. Then I am afraid of my abilities as a father being inferior to my wife's as a mother. Even when we are united in a goal, our anxieties derail us from properly accomplishing God's task.

Marriage is an attempt to overcome separation with just one person. We even get to choose that person. But overcoming separation is so difficult sometimes. We might even be able to see the goal in front of us and yet not accomplish it. Our fear or shame creep in. This can happen outside marriage too. We can make friends and actively work toward the same goals, but the relationship crumbles. We hit a wall where we are unable to express ourselves properly, and at the end of the day there is no uniting purpose and method to force a reconciliation. Because there is no forced or enforceable unity, we choose not to be vulnerable because of fear and shame. We are left with separation between all persons, some less and some more.

CHAPTER 3

SEPARATION FROM NATURE

———

"Cursed is the ground because of you; through painful toil
you will eat of it all the days of your life."

Genesis 3:17

Separation from nature began with God's curse against Adam, as
quoted above. I want to begin by defining nature (for our purposes) as
everything non-human and non-spiritual. This includes plants, animals,
minerals, the planets, the stars and everything in between, even things
man-made. While this definition is far-reaching, we will be narrowing our
focus of nature to the piece we have been given governance over, planet
Earth.

The separation of nature is perhaps the most underappreciated. Many
of us no longer really understand what it is to connect with nature correctly.
On one end of the spectrum, we have those who worship nature, and on
the other end, those who abuse nature. Perhaps Adam taught his sons how
to coexist with nature, but we have lost much of this ability. Now, we have
to cultivate the ground, which means there was a time we didn't have to
cultivate the ground.

What was life like before we had a need to plan for the change of
seasons, before the Earth simply provided for us? I imagine life in the
garden not to be free from burden, but a place of satisfaction. I imagine
a place where man cultivated the Earth, but not the way we do today

with farms and storehouses. There would have been no need for farms or storehouses. Humanity's needs would have been satisfied, and the cultivation would have led to the needs of nature being satisfied. Think about it this way. If we were hungry for strawberries, you would find a strawberry bush provided by nature. You might move the strawberry bush to a better location, so animals could just as easily eat and be nourished by it. This is the kind of cultivating I mean – not planting the strawberry bushes in a row, so we might have abundance, but so the bushes would serve the needs of all. This may sound chaotic; but it would not be, because we would have a deeper fundamental understanding and connection with nature. In fact, we would be working to bring order out of the chaos of the planet providing for us. This kind of cultivating allows nature to be in submission to us, instead of us having to dominate nature. Now, instead of nature just providing things, like food, we must spend the majority of our days thinking about and working towards food.

I cannot imagine what the world would look like if we shaped it based on its needs and our desires instead of our needs simply to be met. Yet, our separation with nature enforces us to wonder where our next meal will come from. This drives conflict into the other separations. People with less seek more, and those with more seek to hold what they have and even grow it further. Nature, however, is designed to meet our needs and still does. Nature just no longer shapes to our desires willingly.

FEAR OF THE CREATED

We are poor at faith. Instead we are fearful. We did not trust God, so we ate the forbidden fruit. We do not trust each other, so we are suspicious and aggressive. We do not trust ourselves, so we are insecure. We do not trust nature, so we are greedy. Greed is the divide between us and nature. Greed is ultimately the desire to have more than enough, and it is based on the fear that there will not be enough. It is a fundamental distrust in God's design of nature. It is a well-founded fear. We have all experienced hunger. We have all experienced our needs not being met. Nature bears the brunt of our fears because nature easily should be under our control. However, now we must fight and work to control nature because of our transgressions (Genesis 3:17).

Work is a good thing. It provides purpose and appreciation in life. Yet, God did not intend for us to work this hard in order to eat. Because of our curse, and the great effort required, we have sought ways to lessen the load. This lessening of the load is a good thing, as it frees us to accomplish things that we were always meant to accomplish. But we do not do those things. We do not care for nature with our extra time. We spend our extra time lessening the load more and more until we have the maximum amount of free time, and then what? There is no giving back. We keep lightening our load, so we can eventually have no load. This is when we have hoarded enough resources for a lifetime. How did we hoard so much? By stripping nature of its resources. You see, to reach a certain level of freedom, our greed and therefore fear must be so out of proportion that we actually harm the land from which we received our resources. Then what?

Nature fights back. Famine, hurricanes, and earthquakes are natural products of our abuse of nature. We deforest an area, only to increase the heat of the atmosphere by driving and consuming too much fuel and energy, so environmental disasters are stronger and more devastating. We mine the depths of the earth, only to be surprised when the earth shifts to fill the gaps.

The Earth has been designed to maintain itself for our benefit. Nature reacts to us. Instead of seeking harmony and the betterment of nature, we abuse and misuse it for our own greed. Nature treats abuse with abuse. We should not be surprised by this. Isaac Newton appropriately formulated every action has an equal and opposite reaction. We can only expect from nature what we have done to it. If we strip resources, then eventually nature will reset itself or cease to be, as we have treated it.

Consider the dog. The dog happens to be the perfect example of what man can do with nature. Every kind of dog we have today has been bred by man for a specific purpose. I want to consider three specific dogs over the rest of this chapter. Their names are Spike, Lucky, and Graham, and we will begin with Spike.

Spike is a pit bull, a powerful and strong companion. He is loyal to a fault. He has been bred to be a fighter, and he excels at this. Pit bulls are the dogs you want at your side when you are outmatched by a bear, a pack of wolves or a gang of humans. Spike would not just fight anyone, though. His owner must help him to express those traits. Spike's owner mistreats him to make him meaner and crueler. He frequently beats him, and he feeds Spike only when he wins fights. This makes Spike fearful of his owner and everything else. Spike never attacks his owner, but he is quick to put everything else under his paw. He is vicious toward everything but his owner. These are the traits that make Spike dominant in the ring, other dogs do not stand a chance. Eventually, though, Spike gets old and his injuries catch up with him. He starts losing fights and gets hungrier and hungrier. Then this cruel dog acts against his equally cruel owner.

In this example, after enough time, cruelty, and abuse, nature will act against us, even though it is we who ought to be in control. Our own cruelty is reflected back to us by nature. I think we so often fear nature because we fear ourselves.

APATHY OF NATURE

Most of us are not cruel to nature. The majority just do not care, and I am in this group. When oil spills in the Caribbean, I am sad, but I am not going to do anything about it. Deforestation of the rainforest does not affect me directly. These are the sentiments often held by the majority of our populace. We simply cannot see how anything matters, outside of a natural disaster presently wrecks us. This is perhaps the most indicative of our separation from nature, our apathy.

In the beginning, Adam named every living creature. Understanding the amount of effort this took is quite difficult. It was not just a parade. In the ancient world, names had much more meaning than they do today. Names were truly a personal descriptor. Knowing this, imagine Adam having to spend time with each animal, understanding their strengths and weaknesses and what makes each animal unique. Then he names them (all of this before Eve, too). Sure, there might have been some easy ones – the dung beetle, for example. But each living creature would have taken time. Think about how connected you would be with all life on Earth if you spent the time to get to know each and every living creature. Imagine the care you would have for each animal and its environment and what it needed to survive and thrive. This is what God intended for us to do to care for our planet.

In our separation from nature, we do not care about what is happening locally, much less globally. This is not to say that we cannot use the planet's resources. It is to say that we could be doing a better job if we collectively cared more.

Let us look at our next dog, Lucky. Lucky is a German shepherd. Lucky is incredibly smart, loyal, clever and strong. Lucky was not bred to fight like Spike, but to herd and protect. The German shepherd has since moved on from simple shepherding due to its incredible intelligence. They are the bomb dogs we are so familiar with. Lucky is owned by an average family in an average neighborhood. Lucky is technically owned by the oldest son, who just turned 16. Patience, discipline and sacrifice do not describe many 16-year-old boys today. Lucky's owner loves her, but he fails to train her and work her very well because there are better things to do sometimes. German shepherds, though, need to be trained and worked. They are too intelligent to just lie down and be pets. Without this training, Lucky will either find another master or will become her own master. Unfortunately, Lucky's owner is too busy playing sports, chasing girls, playing videogames and attempting to be cool. Lucky does not receive the training she needs. Lucky turns out not to be so lucky because she eventually begins to "act out" by getting into pantries, closets, and bathrooms and causing a mess. Because the owners do not care enough to realize what Lucky is communicating, they deem her untrainable and not fit for house life. They ship her off to the pound where hopefully she will receive the direction her life needs.

Can we ship off Earth because we deem it "untrainable"? If we could, should we? Of course not! This world is ours to subdue. We should not leave it alone. We must care enough to understand the inner workings of our world.

LOVE OF THE CREATED

Beyond apathy or abuse of nature, many attempt to overcome separation with nature. This group of people is often defined by fighting against those who abuse nature. They heighten public awareness and bring lawsuits against the abusers. They are the first responders to an oil spill, nuclear waste and natural disasters. They fund protection for nature preservations and endangered animals. This funding is not only to fight the abusers, but to call the apathetic to action. With these actions, the separation with nature is overcome. This love, however, is often taken to the extreme, and the true purpose of nature can be lost. While I have focused on the natural so far, the love of the created extends beyond God's creation to what we have created. So even in our infatuation with nature, we find anxiety.

Those who fight vehemently for our planet are often dismissed for their misunderstanding of the purpose of nature. They attempt to elevate nature above its purpose. This purpose is difficult to understand when subduing and having dominion over nature convey such negative experiences. Usually unhealthy dominion is what we see instead of passionate care of and protection for something. Subduing nature means keeping it under human needs and never above. Humanity is meant to control nature, not the other way around. To the lovers of nature, I understand how sometimes you must use shrewd tactics in order to preserve and protect nature for the betterment of us all. For your efforts, I commend and thank you. However, no animal, plant or resource will be more important than a human. The elevation of nature is a good thing when done in moderation and with the correct purpose.

While some have an extreme love of God' creation, many have an extreme love for man's creation. We all like to stand proud of our own accomplishments and build monuments to ourselves. We love our big buildings and our tiny electronics. We love our stuff. We love things we have power. This is part of what created the mess in the first place.

> "For God knows that when you eat of it your eyes shall
> be opened, and you will be like God, knowing good and
> evil." Genesis 3:5

This quote from the serpent to Eve plays on our desire to claim things God's things. Eve desired the Knowledge of Good and Evil. She wanted to be like God, having claim to this knowledge. In the present day, this plays into our materialism, claiming more and more and more. The underlying problem and a major factor in this separation is that most of "our stuff" is not our stuff.

Let me give you an example. Look at your phone. Did you build it? Did you place every wire and processor and circuit in it? Where did those pieces come from? Another factory which makes them? From what? Nature? Who created nature? We only transmute what is already available to us, which came from God. Perhaps, though, you may believe that nature just came to be. So, look at it this way. Did you plant and water the trees in nature?[11] Did you set the mineral composition of the earth? Did you build or do the mining to acquire those minerals? No, you did not do all these tasks. You may argue that by paying for the phone, your part of the process of its construction is unimportant. How did you make your money for buying the phone? Did you create the job on your own? Did you acquire the knowledge your job requires on your own? Did you raise yourself outside of human community? Did you create your own embryo? All of these things required others, and without them you would have nothing. All these things occurring just so you could buy a new phone every year?

The human experience does not exist outside of history. It does not exist outside of Nature. We have been given so much. We can do Calculus because of Sir Isaac Newton, who invented it because the Arabian peoples preserved mathematical knowledge during the Dark Ages and who learned it from the Greeks who learned it from the Persians, Babylonians, Israelites, Egyptians, and on and on. We are a species of knowledge builders; each accomplishment occurs only because we have built on the foundation laid by others. Each individual is unable to lay claim to any particular accomplishment. Humanity is unable to lay claim to the whole of our accomplishments because we did not create the planet on which we live. Our accomplishment is centered around our circumstances and difficulties. Without those difficulties there would be no need for accomplishment. Thus, our whole existence has been at least partly determined by the very planet on which we live, and we did nothing to earn or deserve life upon it. Forgetting this humility is what so often drives a wedge between us and Nature.

Our final dog, Graham, is a championship show hound. He is well-trained, coached, loved and honored. Graham's owner spends a great deal of time with him. Graham is the favorite in the family. The spouse and the children cannot compete, once good friends of Graham's owner become acquaintances. Graham's owner only interacts with Graham and his rivals on the show floor. After living a full life, Graham dies, having won many awards and shows and bringing fame and fortune to his owner. But what does the owner do now? His family and friends are estranged after ten years of neglect. Graham is dead. The owner now realizes his mistake in failing at his priorities. Graham was always a master-class show dog, but he was not a part of the family, and now his owner is not either. Graham's owner is now left with a bunch of stuff. Are you and I any different? I do not have a show dog, but I do have things I mis-prioritize in my life because I love the created things too much.

Our separation anxiety with Nature finds its foundation in our inability to maintain perspective of what actually is ours and actually important. Nothing is ours, a humbling perspective. Staying humble allows us to understand what is important. It is our privilege to love nature, with appropriate perspective.

CHAPTER 4

SEPARATION FROM SELF

"For what I do not do is the good I want to do; no, the evil
I do not want to do - this I keep on doing."

Romans 7:19

Think introspectively with me. Examine yourself thoroughly and you will discover as Paul has in Romans 7 that you cannot control yourself. You will find parts of yourself fighting to satisfy their own needs. The mind seeks a different satisfaction than the body, which seeks a different satisfaction than the spirit. What, then, are the different parts and their purposes, and why are they so rarely aligned?

THE IMAGE OF GOD

A natural place to start would be with our creator. In the creation account of Genesis 1, we can read about how God created and ordered the world. God brought order out of chaos. Toward the end of the first chapter, he creates humans. We get a deeper look into the process when Chapter Two picks up the story. Both chapters point to this important truth, we are made in God's image. God is the blueprint for how we are made. Understanding the makeup of God allows us to understand ourselves better. Even if you do not believe in God, the ancient Biblical text may still provide some insight into how we are composed, whether a deity is involved or not.

> "So God created mankind in his own image, in the <u>image of God</u> He created them; <u>male and female</u> He created them." Genesis 1:27

The Image of God or *Imago Dei* is not a new concept.[12] The *Imago Dei* is our soul. It is all of us summed up. It is our eternal spirit or will, mortal flesh, and our mind. The *Imago Dei* is what separates us from the animals and plants. We have a stronger mind, more adaptable body, and a strong will to accomplish and drive us. God gifted us His image, so we may have dominion over the earth. Without all of the pieces of our soul, we would be an inferior species. Many apes have stronger bodies, yet our mind and will give us superiority. Other animals may be just as clever, yet our bodies give us superiority. Still, should an animal reach us in mind and strength, our collective will cannot be underestimated.

If you do not believe in our collective will, I would direct you to the day of September 11, 2001.[13] On that day, the terrible tragedy of the Twin Towers falling caused an extraordinary event. People prayed. Regardless of denomination or religion, we all collectively hoped and feared for one thing. While prayer may be curious in and of itself, the results of those prayers are far more fascinating. There exists in many computers a random number generator (RNG). This simple program has one job, to continually pull numbers out of a virtual hat. These programs have withstood numerous tests for tampering. They are, in a weird way, a constant on which computers and many programs can run. Yet, on September 11 day with so many humans praying and utilizing the only thing they could, their will, something interesting happened. The RNGs stopped being random. In fact, they started outputting elegant sequences of numbers. You may think this was limited to one computer, and it just got lucky or particularly affected by the collapse of the economic computers. But computers across the country and even around the world began to output similar sequences. Not only were they not random, they were not random together. Our will can change the very laws of reality. Constants can no longer be true.

The Image of God was gifted to us to have dominion over the earth. Imagine being so in tune with others and yourself that you can alter reality. Luck and chance do not exist for those with a strong enough will. Things simply are. This points back to God's creative ability when God said let there be light, it was so.

If our collective will is so strong, imagine what collective strength or mind bring about. Collective mind brought about the atomic bomb. Collective strength built the pyramids. How much a travesty, then, to lose even one person from the collective? Can we even undervalue a particular person's contribution? Think back in history when a people have been undervalued. Egyptians slaughter Hebrew babies. Stalin slaughters his own people. Americans continue to allow concentration camps. Mass quantities of human death are indicative of an undervaluing of the human soul, and by extension, God.

No one can understand all of God, but He left us clues as to His composition, so we may understand and reflect the same composition. He left us clues throughout scripture, but He left us the most interesting ones right at the beginning so it would not be too hard for us to find the trail of breadcrumbs. Genesis 1:26 talks about God creating humanity, but if you read it carefully, the word used for God is not singular but plural. Who is the plural in verse 26?

"Then God said, "Let us make mankind in our image, in our likeness, so that they may rule over the fish of the sea and the birds in the sky, over the livestock and all the wild animals, and over all the creatures that move along the ground." Genesis 1:26

TRINITY IN GOD

"In the beginning was the Word, and the Word was with God, and the Word was God. He was with God in the beginning. Through him all things were made; without him nothing was made that has been made." John 1:1-3

John 1 points to what is now known as the trinity existing began before everything. In his gospel account, John is referring to Jesus, the first part of the trinity, as the Word. All things were made through him. Jesus is also the part of God that became flesh. Thus, he represents our fleshly selves. But, if there is a trinity amongst God, would He not create a trinity within us as well if is He is to make us in His image? If Jesus is the flesh, then what is the Spirit?

Let me give you evidence of what I mean when I speak of the Spirit or Holy Spirit, which is the second part of God. The ancient Hebrews were well acquainted with the Spirit of the Lord. I find one of the most visible uses of the Spirit of God to exist in 1 Samuel 19. At this point the current king of Israel, Saul, is trying to kill the anointed second king, David. Read the following excerpt of his chase of David.

> When David had fled and made his escape, he went to Samuel at Ramah and told him all that Saul had done to him. Then he and Samuel went to Naioth and stayed there. Word came to Saul: "David is in Naioth at Ramah"; so he sent men to capture him. But when they saw a group of prophets prophesying, with Samuel standing there as their leader, the Spirit of God came on Saul's men, and they also prophesied. Saul was told about it, and he sent more men, and they prophesied too. Saul sent men a third time, and they also prophesied. Finally, he himself left for Ramah and went to the great cistern at Seku. And he asked, "Where are Samuel and David?"

> "Over in Naioth at Ramah," they said.

> So, Saul went to Naioth at Ramah. But the Spirit of God came even on him, and he walked along prophesying until he came to Naioth. He stripped off his garments, and he too prophesied in Samuel's presence. He lay naked all that day and all that night. 1 Samuel 19:18-24

The Holy Spirit is no joke in this passage. Saul and three bands of soldiers fail to capture David due to the power of the Spirit of God. The Spirit of God just stops Saul and his men. It describes them as prophesying. I imagine Saul and his men received a revelation about the Glory of God, and they could do nothing but prophesy. Prophesying can be like praising God in ways we are familiar, as with song and dance. It is also the speaking of deep truth. The truth is true for all time and all people. This is a difficult thing to understand in our age of skepticism, but I imagine something similar happened to Saul, who became Apostle Paul, on the road to Damascus. The Spirit of God revealed the Glory of God to such an extent where adoration, praise and prophecy are the only responses that Saul could generate. This is why Jesus says later not to blaspheme against the Holy Spirit (Mark 3:29). The Holy Spirit fully reveals the Glory of God.

A third part remains, though – the Father God. While anyone can sense interactions with the Spirit, and anyone can see the ground we walk on and therefore Jesus, the Father is the most difficult to grasp. Noted theoretical physicist, Stephen Hawking, would call this aspect of God the celestial dictator. Richard Dawkins and other agnostics and atheists would have Christians end their relationship with this part of the trinity. This is the part of the trinity full of wisdom and wrath. The Father is He who would destroy the Israelites from Mount Horeb. It is He who is spoken about by Solomon in the Book of Proverbs, Chapter 9 (below). It is He to whom Jesus prays in order to feed five thousand. He is the bookends, the Alpha and the Omega, the almighty and praiseworthy, the living God. Hear O, Israel: The Lord our God, the Lord is One!

> "The fear of the LORD is the beginning of wisdom, and knowledge of the Holy One is understanding." Proverbs 9:10

THREE PARTS OF MEN

If the Lord is in trinity, how are we trinity if we are made in his image? Reexamine Genesis 1:27.

> *"So **God** created mankind in <u>his own image</u>, in the <u>image of God</u> **He** created them; <u>male and female</u> **He** created them."*
>
> *Genesis 1:27*

Notice the verse repeats itself three times, one repetition for each member of the trinity. Perhaps, it was even completed all at once and not in stages. God gave us wisdom. This is what we would call our mind. God gave us his Spirit or our will. God created our physical and fleshly form in male and female – our body. Thus, the Father is present in our mind, the Spirit in our will, and the Son in our body. These are the beginnings of the image of God. They are also the parts to our soul. If we are to understand our own soul's fracturing, we must understand the three pieces into which we are separated.

Think about both God as trinity and man as trinity as similar to the human body. God the Father is like the nervous system. God in Jesus Christ is like the musculoskeletal system. God in the Holy Spirit is like the circulatory system. Combined, they form one being, called God: three parts they appear and function separately; but without any one part, there is no whole.

The three systems of the human body are combined to form one being, whom we'll call Jane. Separate, the systems perform different roles and function in different aspects, but they are not a complete being, Jane, without each other. Jane without a nervous system cannot move, think or feel. Jane without the musculoskeletal system cannot move or accomplish any task. Jane without the circulatory system has nothing with which to feed her other systems because the delivery of both oxygen and food comes through the circulatory system; so, Jane's body cannot properly function. Remember, it is Jane's musculoskeletal system, Jane's circulatory system, and Jane's nervous system. Jane is the whole being. So, how do our different systems function? What do they need and desire? These are the questions we need to answer next.

THE SPIRIT OF MAN

The Spirit of man desires worship. It is the piece of us that longs to worship something. To better understand one another, worship will be defined in the archaic sense. It means *honor given to someone or something in recognition of their (its) merit.* Our spirit desires to both give and receive honor. Our spirit drives us for awards. This honoring is integral to us as a basic need. We will worship something. Perhaps our honor goes to money, another person, a discipline, a deity, or even our own self. Regardless of what it is, we worship something. This drive must be satiated. Like all things, there are two extremes. We can find an over-expressed or under-expressed spirit or will. When under-expressed, we are unhappy, moody and depressed. Depression is the physical response of our spirit being frustrated. This can occur for a variety of reasons. The most common of which I believe is found in worshipping something unworthy. The thing to which we were providing honor was undeserving of our worship or is unfulfilling. The other response to unfulfilling worship is to become the opposite of depressed, zealous.

Zeal, the overexpression of will, is when we take our worship of something too far. To be validated in our worship, we seek to convert as many people to our worship as possible in any way possible. Zeal is interesting because in it the strength of will can be seen most easily. Someone is literally willing you to think as they do. Those around the zealot find their minds being changed without meaning to. The strength of will exerted by the zealous is intoxicating. The will drives us to worship either the person or their idol. The will exerted by this person can take over and be passed on to another person. Do not be deceived, though. Just because the spirit is strong does not make the person or idol better or more right than anyone else.

Look at the spirit of a depressed person. Does it not make those around them depressed? We inherently distrust the spirit of a depressed person. Let me give you an example from the popular *Winnie the Pooh* stories. Think of Eeyore. Do the characters ever listen to what he says? Of course not! They do not trust him because of his sulky attitude, even though he is right most of the time. They end up listening to the overzealous Tigger, who gets them into trouble.

Our spirit, like the other two parts of our soul, needs to be monitored. Our spirit if not in balance will lead us astray. As a bearer of the image of God, whatever you worship receives great importance. You had better make sure it is something worthy of the great honor you will place upon

33

it. Many people worship money, which is why the Bible has over 2,000 verses about it. By contrast, there are about 500 verses on prayer and less than 500 on faith.

THE FLESH OF MAN

The human body is one of the most fascinating things in the world. As someone who has studied biomedical science, I appreciate the intricacies and elegance with which we are designed. It serves a purpose beyond just moving our mind and spirit. It anchors us. At the end of the day we must all eat. We must all sleep. We must all breathe and live and die. Our body is a living testament to the majesty of God's design. Nothing is quite as elegant. Simple in the correct places, but with incredible depth and perfection as needed. Yet because of the body's needs we can lose control.

Our human desires can often get the better of us. How many of you get hangry (angry because of your hunger)? Our ancestors used to seek a way to transcend these "baser" urges. Our forefathers knew well what occurred to men who let their baser or more animalistic urges control them. We lose rationality. We lose pieces of what makes us different from the animals. Our spirit becomes consumed with the need to feed or sleep. Our mind becomes too focused. We are useless. What is right and what is wrong go out the door. The only things that matter are a selfish satisfaction of the urge. Many of us experience this in those hangry moments. Yet think of how our American culture revolves around these urges. In America we gorge on food so much that we have created health problems new to man. One of the most profitable industries in the world, the pornography industry, is based on the need of man to expend himself sexually.

Overindulging is not any more of a sin than withholding. Models seek the perfect human form and, in such pursuit, starve themselves. Athletes in pursuit of greatness take supplements that do harm to their bodies. I applaud physical fitness, but the over-pursuit of human form is as much a base desire as the lack of care for your body. See what Paul has to say about our physical bodies.

> Do you not know that your bodies are temples of the
> Holy Spirit, who is in you, whom you have received from

God? You are not your own; you were bought at a price.
Therefore, honor God with your bodies. 1 Corinthians
6:19-20

Paul is specifically referring to the sexual desire of the Corinthians, but we can apply the deeper truth to a multitude of situations. Paul is telling us not to succumb to our baser desire because our body is a temple to God. He reminds the Christians that we were bought at a price. We must remember to honor God with our bodies neither neglecting nor over-honoring our bodies.

Our bodies are what tie us into space. A mind may transcend space. A spirit may last an eternity. Our bodies last only about 80 years. We must care for them, but not in the same way we care for our spirit or mind. Our body must be kept fit and clean, so our mind and spirit may not be obstructed in honoring God. For without self-control over the body, my mind and spirit cannot accomplish much. Without my body, I could not write this very book to communicate the wonders of the Lord. A balance must be struck. Yet, we are out of balance. Too often we consume without thought. Too often we expend more energy than needed on our bodies. Too often we allow our bodies to control us.

THE MIND OF MAN

If our spirit is so strong, then what is the point of a mind? If we often succumb to our baser urges, what can our mind do? When I think of great minds throughout history, I think of Socrates, Aristotle, Hippocrates, Caesar, Imhotep, Sun Tzu, Confucius, Locke, Hobbes, Voltaire, Adam Smith, Thomas Jefferson, Karl Marx, C.S. Lewis, Bill Gates, and Stephen Hawking. What a history we have due to these minds! How much wider is the human experience because these men honed their spirit into iron and pushed past the baser urges to the wisdom of their mind. Truly, Hawking is a great example of mental fortitude in the face of a degrading body due to ALS. These men had minds that cut through time. They are remembered by our minds because of the strength of theirs. The human mind is our history. We build upon those past minds to forge the future. They are our foundation. Our brains are by far more complex than any computer imaginable. Such a complex organ is needed to house such a complex system. The mind is where we find wisdom. It feeds on knowledge. It is a powerful thing when exercised. Yet, a mind is not perfect. The mind is vengeful. The mind remembers.

Our mind can drive us just as our spirit or body can. Our mind can shove aside our baser urges. It can quell our spirit. An underutilized mind allows the spirit and body to fight for control without much thought. There is no care beyond the next meal or next passion. In some ways we know this to be a simpler life, though I do not think many of us would choose it. This type of mind wastes away, only seeking the benefit of the body and spirit. It is not a mind for God.

The over-honored mind is highly prized among humanity, for we know it holds wisdom ours does not. Yet, the mind is vengeful and is quite capable of committing atrocities our body and spirit may not. The over-honored mind becomes paranoid. Our minds are always aware that there is more to know, but a soul controlled by the mind finds the unknown to be a threat. Threat expands into people and eventually becomes a lonely mind. The mind being so lonely is a quite frightening place to be. Information is not shared and becomes wasted. All of the minds I listed a few paragraphs ago sought to share information. They appropriately have used their minds to convey what others do not know. They shine light into the mysteries of the world. Yet, how easy is it to fall into paranoia or lack of exercise.

The mind seeks growth and knowledge, which is what we call wisdom. The mind consumes the most knowledge in times of peace. In peace, the mind can converse with other minds normally separated by conflict. In war, however, our minds are tested to see if the knowledge we gained was sufficient or useful.

Imagine a chess player. The player studies chess moves and matches. As they study, they grow learning from masters and mentors. How much and the relevance of that growth is only known when challenged to a match. The conflict tests our studies. Did we study the correct thing? Did we study enough? Our minds fluctuate between a need for peace and for war.

Those who prize their minds find themselves suspicious and untrusting. Our mind hammers the spirit and the body into form in order to spar and test itself against other minds. Our mind seeks superiority. We know there is one greater than us. We feel the need to prepare to face him. We seek the knowledge he kept from us, even though it was for our benefit. Our mind led us down the path of destruction. While a mind is a terrible thing to waste, it is also a terrible thing to behold and be subject to. Our mind cannot surpass the one who made us, as a computer cannot surpass our mind. Thus, our mind's ultimate fear is often confirmed – there is infinitely more to learn and more than our body or spirit can handle.

THE ANXIETY INSIDE

The struggle for control within our soul is split three ways. The spirit seeks worship, the body seeks desire, the mind seeks wisdom. The anxiety in man comes from these three pieces attempting gain control. They do not function in harmony. They are rarely in agreement, and so we expend our energy working to satisfy them individually or in suppressing one or two for the sake of the third. We are not free to work in true harmony. We cannot achieve our full purpose. Of course, there are great men and women who unified themselves by hammering the other two pieces into the need of the third. Do not be fooled, though. it is not a true unity. A true unity would occur when all sides have their needs met.

Think of it this way. We consider a good compromise when all sides walk away with some needs met and some needs unmet. An old quote captures the sentiment, "A good compromise is when everyone agrees but walks away unhappy." This is the "unity" we settle for inside. Our soul cries out for unification, but we remain unable to create singular purpose. Our singular purpose is generated externally, and we remain separated from the one who can give us true purpose to unify and satisfy our soul. As the saying goes, "you must first love yourself before others can love you." Love is a unifying factor that can cause the parts of the soul to function in harmony.

CHAPTER 5

SEPARATION FROM GOD

Then the man and his wife heard the sound of the Lord God as he was walking in the garden in the cool of the day, and they hid from the Lord God among the trees of the garden.

Genesis 3:8

How silly can we be? Adam and Eve had fellowship with a being who knows and created everything. Adam knew this perhaps even better as Eve came from Adam. God knew about our mistake. He knew the instant it happened. He is integral to the whole universe, and the universe broke with our sin. You have seen that we have become separated from each other, from nature, and even from inside our own self. God felt the universe break, and we tried to hide from him in the trees.

This separation from God ought to be the most heartbreaking, but most of us do not even understand a piece of the relationship we had with God and how we have chosen a different path. Make no mistake: we chose this separation. Some would say this was a natural step in God's plan. For them, God always meant for us to arrive at the Fall. To reach true maturity, we had to eat of the fruit. I heavily disagree with this because it still shifts blame from us to God. I think God knew the possibility of our disobedience. He had plans in place should we eat of the fruit. I think he had plans had we never eaten of the fruit.

Others would ask why God even gave us the ability to choose or gave us the choice. They look at all the terrible things of the world and ask why would God not just destroy us? To understand our separation from God, we must at least begin to understand the value he places on free will. At the beginning and the end, we are simply soil and life.

FREE WILL

Free will is perhaps one of the most important Christian tenants. It is rarely talked about and often mishandled. I have often failed to understand what free will is. However, the older I get, the more I can feel and see God at work. He is always at work, and I imagine a large amount of effort goes into maintaining free will for everyone all the time. In my opinion, it is perhaps the real reason Christ was sent to us. But before I get into Christ's purpose, we must understand the nuts and bolts for the concept of free will.

In Genesis 2:7, God describes a fundamental structure of man. Man is both part of the created and part of God. Last chapter we spoke of what the soul is, and the argument still stands, as a soul does *not necessarily* have the free will about which we are talking. Angels, for example, are souls (they have a mind, body and spirit) who do not possess the free will we do. Genesis 2 describes the building blocks or physical reminders of our free will. The soil is the first part. It grounds us in the created, and we are part of the created because of the use of soil. This is the part of man capable of choosing "not God." It is the option to choose us, Earth, and all creation. I am not intending to cast not God in a negative light, for God proclaimed everything created "good," which is in essence not negative. Though it does pale in comparison to the other option, which is God. God's breath of life is what allows us to choose God. So, free will consists of the option: God or not God (the created).

So now that we know what free will is and what it consists of, the choice between God and not God. The question becomes is why God cares so much about it? The discussion usually begins with a misunderstanding of what free will is.

Free will is often handled in the following manner.

39

"If God is so good, how can he allow evil in the world?" The response is thus, "It was man's choice to allow evil into the world via free will." "Then how can he allow free will?" is the response in turn.

The average Christian has a number of responses for replying to this, but they all ultimately boil down to "He is God and I am not, so I do not understand." This is often quite unsatisfactory for the questioner. The problem in this conversation is subtle. It is equating the choices presented in free will with those aligned in good or evil. As previously discussed, the definitions of good and evil often change based on perspective. Equating a changing perspective with an unchanging one is foolish. Since God is unchanging, the choice presented by free will does not change. You cannot always equate the choice presented by free will with the choice of good and evil because the definition of good and evil change. The choice of good versus evil and free will may line up but not always, so they are separate entities. Once separated, we can properly expose why God cares so much for it.

Our purpose is tied up in our ability to choose. Humanity is only unique in our free will. The question of why the choice exists could be simply and equally rephrased as to why humanity exists. The answer to our purpose lies in our uniqueness, we are here to exercise our free will. We are here to choose between God and not God. All the other questions which philosophers have ever had are ultimately tied to this purpose. When we understand our part in free will, which is to use it, we must shift our attention back to God.

What does God get out of this? Why does He expend a great deal of energy maintaining the balance of free will and creating opportunity for us to choose Him or not, even to the point of sending Himself down to earth to die on a cross, so we may have life and live it to the full (John 10:10)? I think the answer is ultimately somewhat selfish in nature. God wants to have real relationships. He wants to love us and us to love Him. We know the only way that love is real is if the other partner has an option to leave, an option to not choose us. So why is free will important to God? Because He wants the love to be real. He designed us to have the choice. In the beginning, we chose to leave, not God. However, He did not leave all of us forever and without the ability to choose Him. He sent himself down to earth, so until the end of time, we would have the option to choose Him.

DOES GOD EXIST?

While clearing up free will may help some, perhaps a more pertinent question many have is: Does God exist? First, there are many good books providing a more complete discussion on this matter. However, it is important to discuss this question. After all, it would be quite difficult to have angst with something non-existent.

Let us take the logical approach. Can you see, hear, touch, smell, or taste God? The answer for some is 'yes' to these, but perhaps for the majority the answer is 'no'. So, our evidence must come from those who have experienced God. Fortunately, we have a book full of people who have experienced God. Beyond those mentioned in the book, we have more who have seen his Son, Jesus. If you believe in what Jesus has to say, then you believe in God. Beyond the historical time period of Jesus, 2000 years ago, others have experienced God. I and many other Christians can attest to the movements of God. You could take our word for it to start, and we could teach you how to see God for yourself. Of course, few if any have actually seen God, but we have seen the impact He has.

If hearsay evidence of millions of people over thousands of years is not enough for you, consider this: Does an electron exist? Of course, it does. But have you ever seen an electron? Do you know anybody who has seen a singular electron? I do not know anyone who has seen an electron, but I still know an electron exists. How? I have seen it experimentally in an Organic Chemistry Lab. I have seen the effects (or impact) of a singular electron. Moreover, I experience the flow of electrons every day when I turn on the lamp in my bedroom, but I have never and probably will never see an electron. How did I know to do an experiment in the Organic Chemistry Lab to demonstrate the existence of an electron? Someone who has seen an electron told someone else, who then demonstrated it experimentally. In the end, though, unless you have done the experiment yourself, you are just taking my word or someone else's about electrons existing. Why are electrons any different than God? If I can show you God and people have experienced him for thousands of years, why are we quick to forget God and accept something that has only been known for less than 100 years?

SATAN

Satan is perhaps the most often used excuse for why we constantly reject God. After all, he is actively seeking to block us from God (1 Peter 5:8). He is also the prince of this world (John 14:30). He would be quite a foe if we were not given the innate ability to defeat him. Satan has no power over us. Thinking that he has power at all is really quite a lie. It comes from a misunderstanding of his purpose.

As a prince, what would God desire Satan's purpose to be? To find the answer, it might help to understand who the kings and queens of this world are. In Genesis 1:26 it says we have dominion over everything in our world. We are the rulers of this world. If we are the rulers and he is the prince, what might his purpose be? Here I think we can look at how God uses him in the book of Job. Satan is used to test the heart and faith of Job. If this is how God used him, His purpose is wrapped up in exposing our hearts before God. From here, we could see his original purpose was to train us. He was to find the faults in our hearts, and instead of allowing us to be condemned and separated, he was supposed to help us return to God. Consider James 1:2. If we consider it joy to face trials, then we are directing Satan back into his intended path.

Yet, Satan is evil in God's point of view (Matthew 13:38-39). He became twisted from his purpose, which was to expose and help us find God. He only sought to expose our hearts for the evil inside them, separating us from God. This is what Satan did in the Garden of Eden. He has always sought this world. He knows he can take it from the true rulers. He is ambitious and cunning, but he is not more powerful than we are. Blaming Satan for our separation from God is as foolish as God blaming Satan for our separation. God will hold Satan accountable for what Satan has control over, and Satan does not have control over us (Luke 10:19). Only we control ourselves.

ANXIETY WITH GOD

So why do we have such anxiety between us and God? The answer is quite simple. We do not like God's ways. We find them misguided and lacking. Thus, we are anxious about following his commands. In the beginning, we felt the pang of our flaws, and so we ate the fruit to rectify this feeling. Instead of seeking perfection in the creator, we traded in the creator for His creation. We do this constantly. We trade in true fulfillment for the creation. Why do we do this? It is because at our very core we find God selfish.

We are unwise in believing our value should somehow allow us to say that God should not be selfish. God's selfishness draws out our sinful nature. Our sinful nature wants things to be fair and equal. It wants things to be "right" and "good" for us, which is only for our own self. Yet, someone being selfish is universally seen as a bad thing. Our spirit cringes when other people are selfish. Our mind rebels in the thought of a being (perhaps other than yourself) is the center of the universe. Our bodies want to be praised and sought after over everything else. So, in attempts to cover our own deficit and elevate ourselves up to the level of God, we ate the fruit so we would have the knowledge of good and evil.

This is why the Bible is so offensive to human nature. The Old Testament is littered with murder and genocide, sanctioned by God. How can a "good" God allow, let alone sanction, such terrible human atrocities? Ultimately, the Bible is a story about a God who is ultimately for Himself, and this selfishness is ultimately a selflessness for his creation. God, gifting us His image, is for His glory but our benefit, because then we can fully live. When we continually fail to represent Him appropriately, the insult to His glory is so great He must cut the piece away. That is hell, the place of existence apart from God.

Think of it this way. If you invent something, is it yours? If you come up with an idea, is it yours? Do not you claim ownership over your invention? I would. God is doing this in His selfishness. He is claiming what He created. He is claiming His stuff. As Image-Bearers, we are His. He created the whole universe. All of it is His. What right do we have to any of it? Only what he allows. But do not you take care of your stuff? Do not you spend time washing your car, repairing your house, loving your children? This is what God does. By choosing God, you are actually choosing a better existence for yourself. We are separated, though. Trusting in God does not seem right, even though the wisest man told us, "There is a way that seems right to man. In the end it leads to death." Our lack of trust is why there is such anxiety between God and us. Those who overcome this distrust find God a privilege to love.

THE CRUX OF THE SITUATION

If God is love and we are made with the ability to choose God, then we can choose love. Therefore, it is our privilege to love unlike anything else. This allows our nature to be quite mutable. Think about God. He cannot be angry or spiteful or vindictive for no reason or seek the world into destruction "just because." He is always love and always will be. This may lead you into a path of thinking of God as lesser or weaker or has no choice regarding things. One without wisdom may argue, "God created a rock he could not lift when he made us." Since he is immutable, are we not more powerful? The answer is, of course, 'No'. The point of our privilege is that He might have the same privilege. God chooses us. His options in free will both lead to His own glory. Each choice lasts eternally, unlike our two options. Yet they remain similar in essence. His options are more focused: He can choose the easy way (Himself), or the more difficult but more rewarding path of choosing us. Either way God ultimately chooses His own glory. Our free will opens up His free will.

He is constantly having to choose us. This is why it seems his mind can be changed. This is how the fathers of our faith converse boldly with God. Abraham argues for the cities of Sodom and Gomorrah (Genesis 18:22-33). Moses intercedes for the people of Israel (Exodus 31:11-14). The story of Hosea is a metaphor for God choosing us over and over. Finally, the cross is where He chose us to the fullest extent. He chose us so much that He died on a cross. He cannot stack the deck for us to choose Him any more than by coming down and showing us how to choose a relationship with Him. God chooses unification with us. What we will choose, unified peace or separation anxiety.

PART 2

CHAPTER 6

UNIFIED PEACE

While facts describe the first part of the book, faith characterizes the second part. The first part shows a faith is rooted in objective fact. The second part shows how it takes faith to overcome our separation anxieties and find a unified peace. You must have faith in Christ to reach unified peace.

Peace, for our purposes, is defined as freedom from dispute or dissension between individuals or groups. The word "unified" is rooted in the word "unify", which is defined as, "to make into a unit or coherent whole." In many ways these are the exact opposite of separation and anxiety. This means we can counteract the anxiety brought about by separation with finding peace in unity. If we are to move beyond our separation anxiety and take hold of the fullness of life, then we must enter into a unity brought about by peaceful interactions with those things from which we are separated. For each separation we must re-attach ourselves in the appropriate manner.

The measure of our unification is directly related to the measure of peace we hold. If I submit to God, then we have peace and therefore unity. If I am self-controlled, then I am at peace with myself and have found unity. If nature and I work in peace, then we are unified. If I am peaceful with my wife, then we are unified. This is in direct contrast to separation anxiety. The amount of separation we have is measured by our anxiety levels.

Momentary peace is frequently achieved. Our circumstances are always in flux, and therefore a peace is difficult to maintain by even those who work hardest at it. Ultimately, to achieve this peace we ignore one or more of the separations. For example, medieval Christian monks withdrew from the world to achieve unity with God and self, but ignored unity among men.

While God may be found momentarily in the lonely places, we are always driven to share God with other men in attempts to overcome our own separation from men and their separation from God. Buddhist monks may attempt to divorce the conflict of self to achieve a unity within, and by doing so achieve a unity with other men or nature or a god. These examples are not a true peace and lasting unification which can only be found in one man.

Jesus the Christ is the man, who is God, sent to provide a method of overcoming our separation anxiety and achieve unification through peace. Unified peace begins with finding reconciliation with God and ends in solidarity with God. The other peaceful unifications are fueled by the peace we obtain from God through Jesus. The question is, though, who is this Jesus that we should call him Christ and learn how to obtain peaceful unification? In short, the answer is Jesus is God's continual display of His desire to have peace with us. He sacrificed himself for us, and now we can appreciate a unified peace with God, ourselves, nature and other men.

WHO IS JESUS?

If Jesus is the method for obtaining unified peace, then a pertinent question would be: "Who is Jesus?" Many often have interactions with two whom they call "Jesus". The first Jesus is someone they intellectualize and who lived over 2000 years ago. This man is a historical figure to them, just as they would understand Julius Caesar, Socrates or Plato. The second Jesus is a present-day realization that he is real and present in our lives. Both are the same Jesus. It bears repeating, the historical Jesus is the same Jesus as today. Again, there is no distinction between the Jesus we read about in the Bible and the Jesus we encounter today.

I can only discuss this modern-day Jesus honestly by using one method.

I must tell you who Jesus is to me. I can only do this by telling my story and showing you where Jesus is in my story.

Before I begin my story, I must repeat our new growth beyond objective fact in faith. Here we must begin to trust. Before now, this book has argued from objective truth, and it still will, but faith will be required to continue if you want to fully understand this work. Do not be concerned if you doubt or cannot have complete trust right now. Just look for Jesus in my story. By telling my story, I am sharing my faith or trust with you. This means the burden of faith is not completely on you. I will help you carry some of it, and others will help you too, if you allow them. Jesus will carry much of the burden for both of us.

MY STORY

I grew up going to church. As a child, my parents did not seem have great faith, but they were wise enough to make church and God a priority. They certainly believed in the facts of Jesus and always have. Tithing, smart finances, Christian living, and the Bible as a source of wisdom were all impressed upon my brother (younger) and me. However, I did not know if my parents ever really trusted God with a lot growing up. They trusted in themselves and a strong work ethic much more. What this meant to me was that God was real, and only fools doubted His existence. God was the one who knew the rules, and if you wanted success, you followed His rules. Sometimes those rules might not make sense, but success was always found in following them. While this is certainly a beginning of faith, it is not much more than what the Pharisees of the New Testament practiced. Note, Jesus is here with my parents. He guides them to set our family up for success in faith. It is neither me nor my parents who do anything to build this foundation. It is Jesus working before I was born and while I was a child.

The cementing of my faith foundation occurred in June 1999. Something hit me during the sermon that Wednesday night. Looking back, I can only remember scant details, but the ones I do are engraved on my heart. It was a hot day in Birmingham, Alabama. We were new to the city, having just moved for my father's work. The sun was setting as the preacher spoke on Isaiah 6. What I remember about the scripture is how it affected me so greatly that I began sobbing in church. As a 9-year-old in my family, I knew the rule, "men do not cry," and every 9-year-old boy wants desperately to begin the passage into manhood. Crying in public would certainly bar me from acceptance. I had thought tears and emotion had been stamped from my being by now, yet here I was with tears draining from my eyes in the middle of church! I remember fighting the urge to sniff loudly, the inevitable snot that comes from a good cry because the sound would have drawn too much attention to me. Instead, I opted to catch what I could with a hand and wipe it inside my cargo shorts (which I am sure confused my mom on laundry later that week). Thankfully, the sermon ended shortly after, so I was able to escape to a restroom and compose myself. From the experience, I knew it was time to do the Jesus thing for real and get baptized.

In the church in which I grew up, knowledge of the Bible was equated with being a good Christian. As someone blessed with good intellect, it was simple enough to just pay attention and know my placement among my peers. I did none of the "bad" stuff and did enough good stuff to fly under the radar of "kids to watch." Later, in the 8th grade, Jesus had me fall in love with the woman who is now my wife. After a high school experience of one or the other liking each other, we found ourselves in college together: her first choice, my safety school. I am convinced much of my tiny little faith today is due to my parents deciding to raise me in church and my spending four short years at Lipscomb University. There are very few places on earth where you can learn Evolutionary Biology, Spanish, Physics, Business and Bible from men and women who love God. Lipscomb built a fortress of faith on the foundation my upbringing had already laid. I have never lacked any knowledge because of my time at Lipscomb, which was all by the grace of God.

After Lipscomb, my wife and I moved to Chicago, and I learned of faith beyond knowledge. Before Chicago, I thought there was little to learn beyond how to advise and lead others to Christ. Now, I know how small my faith is. My faith moved from a classroom to the real world. The question was not "Is there a God" or "What does He want you to do?" The question was "Do you trust God in every situation?"

You see, it is easy to trust God when you are in a fortress. You are protected by lifetimes of knowledge and experience, but God and maybe

Lipscomb never asked me to be in a fortress and play defense. God asks me to play offense, to take the fight to the enemy, for He and I are much stronger than our foe. Perhaps what Lipscomb meant to build in me was a tank (a mobile fortress), but I was not mature enough then to see it. My time in Chicago changed me. Outside of the safety of the Bible belt, where there is quite literally a church every mile or less, I was called into the battle.

When I expressed to my wife the desire to join the High School ministry, I thought I was growing our defensive capabilities. We were already good at church infrastructure, and there is little more integral to the church than its children. We were semi-cool because we were young (22 years old) and relatable, so I thought it would be easy to connect with the teens and guide them along their walk with Jesus. I quickly realized how there was no defense to be played in this ministry.

We inserted ourselves in a time of rebuilding, and you know how they say, "the best defense is a good offense." So, we went with that idea. We wanted to reach a group of kids had grown up in church, but no one had ever really reached out to them. On average there were no parents or other adults trying to help these kids find and love Christ. So, we sought these kids out to lay a foundation of faith like my wife and I had.

What we did was something different. In the process of laying a foundation similar to ours, we began to question whether how we grew up provided the best possible outcome. What we found was our upbringing was a good, maybe even great path, but it was not the best path. So, we tried to meet our teens where they were. We definitely gave them a foundation of knowledge on which to rely, like we had received as children. But I hope we also instilled a trust and faith in Jesus to push them outside and beyond their foundation.

My understanding and faith are made more complete because Christ did not need me to defend his church. That is His job, after all. I was complete in being a servant to God.

Servanthood, however, is not God's endgame for me or for many of us. He calls us to be his friend (John 15:14) and eventual co-heirs with Christ (Romans 8:17). My faith is growing right now in the arena of being friends with Jesus.

For me it is quite a radical shift in thinking. All my life I was aiming for a target I was never intended to hit. I have always tried to be the best servant of God by holding onto the most knowledge and knowing him to the utmost a servant could. Now, I must grow beyond a servant into His friend, and I really do not know what the relationship looks like. Do not get me wrong. Serving God will always be important, but how I serve Him will be quite different. It requires something different. As someone who often imagines medieval times for the way God operates, I will use feudal social contracts as a metaphor to further explain.

If God is a King, then early in my faith I operated as a child in His kingdom. Next, as a teenager I began to apprentice men and women of the kingdom. As an adult, I learned how to serve, but not as anyone of importance. I simply served the servants, not someone who was known. A position like your average guardsman of the castle comes to mind-faceless and unknown to most. Then I became part of the army, going out on expeditions. Now I am working toward knighthood. The King would know who I am as a knight and at least have a deeper relationship because He would have to knight me after all. You see, as a servant I already know Him and what He wants. As a knight, He would be sending me on specific missions or leading troops into battle. The King needs someone to befriend, and who better than His friend the knight who seeks to accomplish His will in the manner in which He would have it done. The knight still serves the King, but it is even more by choice and born out of a deeper and longer relationship with the King.

THANKS FOR THE STORY?

So, you might be wondering what all this has to do with who Jesus is. The truth is, everything and only a small part. Jesus is the author and perfecter of our faith. He is the one who wrote this story, and we can learn a lot about the author of a story by how He writes. So, my story is filled to the brim with Jesus because I keep inviting Him to write it. The foundation in which I grew up, the woman I love, the college I attended, the first experience living away from home, and now returning home to work to become a friend of Jesus. All of it has Jesus in it. The love, the struggle, the work, the failure and the success all have Jesus attached to the story.

Jesus is someone who wants to challenge us, grow us, work with us, love us, talk with us, befriend us, and ultimately admire us. He is our secret admirer. He is the craftsman who steps back from His work and marvels at its sight. In us, He has started a good work. He lived, breathed and died, so we could be worthy of glory. Why, you may ask? So, our peace and unity with God may bring Jesus glory. We are all worthy of glory, just as I am, because we all have God inside us. We can either reject or accept the God part of ourselves.

WHERE WE MEET THE FALL

Jesus is where we reset our relationships from the Fall. He shows us what is possible in a sinless existence. He shows us the extent of our fallen nature. My story helps demonstrate where I meet the fall. It takes theory and theology and becomes practical. Jesus is not spirit but flesh and bone. By following His example, we can overcome our separation anxieties and find a lasting unified peace. This is not a knowledge to hoard to yourself. Jesus is meant to be expressed. We are challenged to meet the fall and win. Jesus tells us the Gates of Hell cannot withstand the advance of Christ. The believer in Christ is unstoppable because peace is so attractive. Christ calls us to abide in His peace. Christ meets us in the Fall. We are not alone. If God is with us, who can prevail against us? The separation anxiety is not meant to be lasting. It is our choice when to end it. Christ the one who unites us to tackle the same problem. Hell cannot stop us from bringing peace in.

UNITY IN CHRIST

The purpose of Christ is to bring us unity, not uniformity. Do you understand the difference? Unity allows for and perhaps encourages individuality, because the best way to solve any problem or reach any goal is to approach it from multiple perspectives and strengths.

Uniformity, though, strips away individuality. It demands each problem or goal be tackled in the same way. The only thing creating separation in uniformity is proclivity and tenacity.

Unity and uniformity differ from the idea of peace as well. A united approach encourages experimentation, changes in theory, and adaptability.

It allows each person to arrive at peace in their own time and their own way. Peace is a state in which many may join in, and it is ever changing, based upon the individuals residing in the state. Uniformity exchanges peace for order. To the uniformist, peace can only be arrived at in a specific manner. Peace must look the same in all, or there is no peace. Christ did not come to us to create a uniform approach to being saved. He came to know each of us individually, so we may all have purpose according to our individual strengths, not just to our proclivity or tenacity in a singular method. Of course, it is true proclivity and tenacity are desired by Christ, but He prescribes these to the methodology of a body. An ear may do its job correctly every time with great strength, yet Christ would not force the ear to be an eyeball or a hand.

The point is this: the call of Christ is to unite underneath him, not to uniform underneath him. In the call, we are able to unite uniquely with God, with ourselves, with nature and with each other. By following in this unity, we will find a peace impossible to come by elsewhere.

CHAPTER 7

UNIFICATION WITH GOD

"Shalom" is the word some Jews use to greet each other. The literal and raw definition of this word means "peace be with you." The literal definition, however, lacks completeness. The greeting evokes more emotion. Commonly, the phrase is used hopefully to mean peace be between you and God. This was because the Jews knew if you had peace between you and God, everything else would fall into place. Jews have used this greeting before and after Christ because there was no way of knowing whether there was peace between you and God. In Jewish understanding, fear and doubt existed in the relationship one could have with God. You may have worked hard and been at peace with the self, nature and others, but there was always an unease about your standing with God. How could they know? For centuries, the only ancient Jew who spoke to God was the High Priest, once a year, unless a prophet came to tell them whether or not they had erred. This is no longer the case, because Jesus came to be a High Priest for us. Now, we may commune with God daily. Jesus leaned into the centuries of tradition which had carried its own form of assurance. He came to bring about a true peace through unification with God by using the foundations already laid.

Like the Jews, we need to understand a peace between God and us allows for everything else to fall into place. However, this is most difficult to achieve truly because we must unite with a being we cannot see, smell, hear or manipulate. This is quite unlike the other separations, over which we all have at least some power. Regardless of its difficulty, unification with God is the most important. When there is no peace with God, we cannot maintain a unified peace with the other separations. This is because God is in all things because all things are made through Him. Through God the separations are overcome because he is the common denominator. Without Him we may stumble upon a denominator within ourselves, with nature or with others. However, the terms are ever shifting because it is in our nature to separate, to classify, and to find differences between things. We are driven to make distinctions. We need to locate our denominator or foundation on something unchanging, and the only thing I know that does not change is God. Without God, continually identifying the common thread is impossible because the only common thread present might be God.

So, what does it mean to unify with God? It means accepting Jesus by faith and living the faith out in obedience. First comes accepting Jesus by faith. While we have little to grasp onto for God the Father, Jesus was a man of flesh and blood. I have already introduced you to the Jesus I know. You can know him in your own way by accepting him as Lord by faith. Why is Jesus central? Because he said so, "No one shall come to the Father except through me" (John 14:6). If we are to have a relationship with Jesus as Lord, then we must respect what He says to us. For many of us, we are ready to accept Jesus as a moralist or even as savior, but to reach a level of peace with God we must accept Jesus as Lord. This leads us to the second point: living faith out in obedience. James argues this in James 2:18-26.

> But someone will say, "You have faith and I have works."
> Show me your faith apart from your works, and I will
> show you my faith by my works. You believe that God is
> one; you do well. Even the demons believe—and shudder!
> Do you want to be shown, you foolish person, that faith
> apart from works is useless? Was not Abraham our father
> justified by works when he offered up his son Isaac on the
> altar? You see that faith was active along with his works,
> and faith was completed by his works; and the Scripture
> was fulfilled that says, "Abraham believed God, and it was
> counted to him as righteousness"—and he was called a

friend of God. You see that a person is justified by works and not by faith alone. And in the same way was not also Rahab the prostitute justified by works when she received the messengers and sent them out by another way? For as the body apart from the spirit is dead, so also faith apart from works is dead.

James is telling us how our faith is visible by what we do or live. Certainly, we cannot be justified by works alone. We need faith in Christ. However, we prove our faith by what we do. We must act to be unified with God. Because this is difficult to understand, we will explore some of the process of unifying with God and how to access the unifying presence of God through the Holy Spirit.

MECHANICS OF UNIFICATION WITH GOD

I begin this section with a disclaimer. God is incredibly creative. He works through unique people uniquely. The mechanics listed below are events, decisions or actions we can take to be unified with God. These mechanics will be listed in a logical order, but certainly I know people who have moved around in this list. I jump through this list in my processes of maturation. So, for those who hate having to go in order down the list, do not feel constrained. For those who like going in order down the list, prepare yourself to jump throughout and to jump off the list of mechanics. All of these mechanics will begin with a Bible verse, and then we will explore the verse for its place in the process of unification with God.

"The fear of the Lord is the beginning of wisdom; all who follow his precepts have good understanding. To him belongs eternal praise" (Psalm 111:10). "The fear of the Lord is the beginning of wisdom" is recounted several times in the Bible, with the exact wording. Since it uses the word "beginning," it is as logical a place to begin as any. When I speak of fear, I include all it entails. I include the fear of being smitten from the Earth. I also include fear in the sense of respect. Perhaps the latter flows from the former, as in my respect for my father, though I once feared the spankings I would receive for doing something wrong. The point of this fear is to begin to realize your position in the world and how big God is. I often think of the realization of how awesome God truly is. No, I do not necessarily mean popular or cool, but in the manner the mountains or the oceans inspire awe. This awe gives us a good cornerstone to be constantly used for reference. In my own maturation, I can think of times when the fear of the Lord was a motivating factor in a good way.

"Blessed are the poor in spirit, for theirs is the kingdom of heaven" (Matthew 5:3). While the previous step was to realize how big God is, this step is to realize how small you are. You are in a weakened and poor state before Jesus, God and the Holy Spirit begin to do some work. Remember, this is a spiritually poor state and not a monetarily poor state, though perhaps it might be easier to admit your spiritual poverty when you have little in the way of possessions. The spiritually poor state activates the knowledge that we need a savior, Jesus.

"For it is by grace you have been saved, through faith – and this is not from yourselves, it is the gift of God" (Ephesians 2:8). You see, as a spiritually poor person, you can receive the gift of grace which is based on nothing you have done. It is a gift from God. He sent His son to sacrifice Himself for you, so you might have a relationship with Him. Jesus, however, is inclusively exclusive.[14] The gift of grace is available to all who claim it, and yet not available to those who do not claim it. How do you claim it? The answer is provided in the verse above – faith.

"And without faith it is impossible to please God, because anyone who comes to him must believe that he exists and that he rewards those who earnestly seek him" (Hebrews 11:6). If the ultimate goal is to be united with God, then it makes sense you would want to please Him, just like you do things to please your friends. Faith in God simply means trusting in Him. The beginning of faith is believing in God's existence. Beginning in faith should be easy if you fear God. You must belief becomes logical because you are afraid of Him. How can you be afraid (long-term) of something non-existant? You must spend the rest of your life choosing to grow in this faith and in your relationship with Him.

I have not come to call the righteous, but sinners to repentance" (Luke 5:32). We are called to repentance. Remember, there is a way that seems right to man; but, in the end, it is folly. Repentance means to turn away from. God desires more than just turning away from sin. It is the turning toward Him. Biblical repentance is not doing what is evil and doing what is good. It is turning towards God and away from what seems right to you. This is not an easy or painless process. I can attest to how difficult it is to repent. Worse yet, I must often repent of the same things over and over, continually choosing God over what I want.

"Through him we received grace and apostleship to call all the Gentiles to the obedience that comes from faith for his name's sake" (Romans 1:5). Next, you must begin obeying Him. The next step is simply living in obedience, which is much easier written than completed. All Christians struggle with obedience. This is where faith is tested. It is often not difficult to ascertain what God wants. It is, however, difficult to follow through. By continually choosing to obey God, you grow in faith and in the love of Christ and you become a disciple.

"Therefore, go and make disciples of all nations, baptizing them in the name of the Father and of the Son and of the Holy Spirit, 20 and teaching them to obey everything I have commanded you" (Matthew 28:19-20). The act of baptism is an important rite of passage in the Christian faith. Baptism is an important in symbol for the individual, and a physical reminder in the literal cleansing of sins. It is also important for the body of believers of which you are a part. It is a public declaration of intent. The declaration of intent has two parts: 1. You have the intent to grow in your faith toward God; and 2. The church will help you along this path. In this way it is similar to a marriage between you and God and you and the Church.

"Peter replied, 'Repent and be baptized, every one of you, in the name of Jesus Christ for the forgiveness of your sins. And you will receive the gift of the Holy Spirit'" (Acts 2:38). At baptism, you receive the Holy Spirit. The Holy Spirit makes things incredibly interesting. If Jesus is the unifier of God and humanity, then the Spirit uses unity to come to us. Jesus says the Holy Spirit is our helper. He even intercedes for us in our prayers. He provides gifts or abilities for the maturity of not just you but the Church body of which you are a part. I will speak more of the Holy Spirit later in the chapter, as it becomes the main method of maintaining unity and peace with God.

"So, Christ himself gave the apostles, the prophets, the evangelists, the pastors and teachers, 12 to equip his people for works of service, so the body of Christ may be built up 13 until we all reach unity in the faith and in the knowledge of the Son of God and become mature, attaining to the whole measure of the fullness of Christ" (Ephesians 4:11-13). In the end, the goal is to become mature, attaining to the whole measure of the fullness of Christ. When you are full of Christ, you will be unified with God, since Jesus Christ is God. The Holy Spirit works on your behalf to make this happen. To attain this maturity, you may have to find yourself poor in spirit again, or learning how to obey, or learning how to fear God again, or doing something else as directed by God and His Spirit. There is a perpetual growth in the Christian life. We continually grow close to God, achieving more peace in our lives. Peace drives away anxiety because we are secure in our relationship with God. There will be periods of doubt, but we can always return to our cornerstone of the awe of God.

These are the main mechanics of how to achieve and maintain unity with God, appreciating the sacrifice Christ made even to allow this unity. It means growing in trust. It also means growing the Holy Spirit inside you.

THE HOLY SPIRIT

So how does uniting with God allow you to maintain peace with the other separations? The answer is the Holy Spirit. By reaching a point of unification with God, you become a recognized disciple of Jesus. You can be baptized and receive the gift of the Holy Spirit. The Holy Spirit allows us to continue to find a common denominator, which powers us to peace and unity instead of all our separation anxiety. For though everything is unique, there is one Spirit (1 Corinthians 12:13). To call Him the glue in the universe would be a massive understatement; however, He does get the train of thought going in the correct direction. More so, the Holy Spirit is a divine mediator. The Holy Spirit is the part of the Trinity acting on our behalf daily. In fact, the Spirit is so involved in our lives that it moves in ways for which we could not even pray. Paul explains it this way in Romans 8:26-27:

> Likewise the Spirit helps us in our weakness. For we do not know what to pray for as we ought, but the Spirit himself intercedes for us with groanings too deep for words. And he who searches hearts knows what is the

mind of the Spirit, because the Spirit intercedes for the
saints according to the will of God.

In this passage, Paul identifies the Spirit as an intercessor. In our
language today, we do not often have use for the term "intercessor". For
the purposes of this writing, a more prudent term is mediator. Mediator
carries the correct connotation while satisfying the denotation of the word
"intercessor". What do you think of when you hear the word mediator?
A quick Google search will likely bring up several divorce mediators in
your area. If a divorce mediator is the most common type of mediator we
have as humans, and we view the Holy Spirit in this light. Then the Spirit
the perfect creation to salve our divorce from God, self, nature and our
fellow man.

The Holy Spirit is how someone maintains a peaceful unity with
everything. How is this possible? Remember, God is Trinity: father (God),
son (Jesus), and spirit (Holy Spirit). Likewise, for us, mind, body, and spirit
make up our soul. If God is the power behind creation, through Jesus, then
the Spirit fills the creation. As Dietrich Bonhoeffer said in his Ethics, "God
is in all of every single blade of grass, yet those blades of grass do not hold
all of God." The Spirit is the part of God filling every blade of grass, every
piece of bark, every fiber of wool on a sheep, and every cell in our body.
It is the role of the Father to be the power supply, the decision maker. It is
the role of Jesus Christ to hold everything together (Colossians 1:17). The
Spirit fills. It is the breath of life. Because God is in all things, we need a
mediator between us and Him to find a lasting unified peace among all
things. We need the Holy Spirit to achieve shalom.

Jesus desired us to have fullness of life (John 10:10). If this is true,
then He meant for us to have the Holy Spirit readily available to us. This
was unlike the Jewish traditions, where the Holy Spirit was only for the
spiritual elite. Jesus wanted the Holy Spirit to be for all. Indeed, Jesus
indicated an advantage in leaving, so the Holy Spirit could come (John
16:17) and fill us (Acts 2:4). While Jesus was with us, He was the last in
the line of spiritual elite. He had to leave for us to receive the gift. Notice,
though, in Acts 2:4, it says the Holy Spirit filled all of them. We often
misunderstand and think the Holy Spirit fills only the apostles, but there
were 120 people with them (Acts 1:15). The Holy Spirit is not just for the

spiritual elite, as evidenced in His first appearance. We may each have fullness of life and no longer be bound by the anxiety of separation. The Holy Spirit is here, so we may find fullness of life through a unified peace.

The Holy Spirit mediates between God and us, meaning God in us and God in everything else. Because the Holy Spirit mediates, we are able to reach agreement. Agreement allows for peace and unity. Peace and unity allow for us all to be focused on a singular goal. The Holy Spirit enhances our own individual talents and traits to reach a goal in the most unified and peaceful way possible.

Remember, to receive the Holy Spirit, we must come to the Father through Christ. It is important to think about these different agencies of God all coming from peaceful unification with a singular being, God. This is how we overcome our separation anxiety. We take steps toward God, who is already working to overcome the separation we have with Him. Upon reaching a peace with God, we are able to use the Holy Spirit to mediate the other separations we have. We become the caller instead of the called. Modeling God's own call to us to reach peace, we achieve shalom in our lives.

WHERE GOD MEETS THE FALLEN

My walk with God has certainly had its ups and downs. Just because I have been a Christian longer than not does mean that God and I are always unified. We have even had a few falling outs over my career failings. Sometimes, what makes a relationship is falling out and coming back together. But, I always keep coming back. I am just stubborn, and God does not require much for you to reach a peace with Him. You just have to stick with Him and keep growing. Here is how I have stuck with him recently.

I was supposed to be a physician. Everyone I have ever met has told me I would be a great physician. I got four degrees in six years and better than needed test scores to get into medical school. I never got in though. I couldn't even get a job in a hospital to increase my chances at future applications. I was not pleased with myself at first, but as I moved further down the list of things to improve my application, I got angry with God. I became aimless and heartless. So, I wrote. Writing is the only safe way I know to work out my emotions. This book started as a frustration. I was angry at following all the rules and not succeeding. So, I wrote a short essay on why the world was broken. What the Holy Spirit did was take those ideas, heal my relationship with God and give me purpose and strength to write this book in a way to praise Him instead of fighting with Him. Through this God and I have found a peaceful union.

God met me where I was, fallen and broken. He used what material there was to reconcile with me. All I had was a couple of ideas on some paper. He reached out and made it more. He is probably reaching out to you right now. God wants to take the fallen and reach a peaceful union again. God finds us where we are. We just have to start into a relationship with Him and other people who have a relationship with Him. In the mechanics section a few pages ago, I hope you can find a place to take some steps to move in a positive direction from our fall. We may not be perfect, but God does not ask us to be. He asks to seek unified peace, *shalom*.

CHAPTER 8

UNIFICATION WITH SELF

Robert Louis Stevenson depicted the idea of separation from self quite beautifully in the fictional work, The Strange Case of Dr. Jekyll and Mr. Hyde. For some the idea of uniting our own self may seem quite foreign to many us. Consider this though, why are there so many self- help books? How can you help yourself if there are not distinct areas of the soul needing assistance? The soul is comprised of the three pillars and the heart. Yet, we cannot find this unity easily or lasting enough to be called peace. Stevenson's novella showed us the lengths someone may go to fight themselves into submission. To reach peace, you cannot fight yourself into submission nor can you separate yourself further the way Dr. Jekyll does in the novella.

Instead, we must embrace and master the parts making us up, but to do so in a Godly way. This is what will bring about peace. For example, Mr. Hyde had a strength and cunning that Dr. Jekyll needed in himself. Instead of embracing it, he suppressed those key parts of himself leading to his eventual death. Remember from our discussion on free will how the struggle of good and evil is not helpful in overcoming separation anxiety. We struggle in unity or disunity with God. Good or evil is of little importance, as God is good. If God is good, then we will naturally find ourselves doing good if we follow Christ. We have to find balance in the soul and allow God to drive the unity in our soul.

To understand the unity in ourselves, we need to look at the unity amongst the Trinity. Since God used himself as the blueprint for our creation, it only makes sense to glean from it. Let us review the conclusions we have come to thus far.

Similar to the Trinity of God, we also are made in trinity. We have mind, body, and spirit. These comprise our soul. Once there was unity in these things, but because sin and death have reached the world, there is disunity. Our bodies decay, while our mind wishes to linger as long as possible and our spirit seeks inspiration. We can fall subject to any one of our trinity. We need to balance them out.

BALANCE WITHIN THE SOUL

The three parts of our soul have unique gifts, talents and purposes. To diminish those gifts and purposes will leave us unfulfilled. Unity in our soul, though, is not accomplished by highlighting the individual part but by highlighting the whole. To use our heavenly example, Jesus works to give glory to the Father, and the Spirit works to glorify Christ, who is then glorified by the Father. They are independently working as a cohesive unit. Each has a role to play, and to not play their role diminishes the whole. The highlighting of the one feeds into the highlighting of the whole. For example, we can praise the feet or the mind or the will of a football player, and the praise will flow from one strength to the next, ultimately resting on the whole player. We say the player is great because of the composite of his parts. A player is not great if he only has strong will, but no size or capability. So, it is within our soul. We are all great players according to our measure and over-emphasizing any part only serves to diminish the whole.

In our soul, our three parts (spirit, body, and mind) must work in unison to achieve peace. In our spirit we must worship a worthy object. God is the only thing that allows us true fulfillment. Certainly, Somethings exist to provide temporary replacement, but worship of God allows our spirit to race as the horse does over the plains. Worship of God also provides us with the bridle to control the spirit into contemplation of His majesty. So, one piece of our soul leads into the next. They feed upon one another in a positive way for the exaltation of the whole.

To worship we need to be presentable in form. God in the Old Testament speaks of the lack of blemish or imperfection to be found on the sacrifices offered to Him. Likewise, our bodies need to be without imperfection. This is impossible to achieve on our own. However, Christ clothes us in his righteousness, so we can be perfect. Does this mean we are free to treat our bodies following any desire? Certainly not! We must beat our bodies into servitude neither over- nor under indulging in anything: food, material fashion, fitness, or sex. Indeed, all these things are good, but should be done in moderation. Just as we are not to allow ourselves to only follow our emotions unbridled, so we are not to follow only bodily needs. We must similarly bridle ourselves, so we may fully enjoy the things of this world. One philosopher said it this way, "By leaning into the hunger, we learn how to hunger for the deeper things. Yes, the way we learn of our hunger for God is to understand our bodily hunger."

To control our hunger and bodily needs, our mind needs steady renewal. Without this renewal the emotions or desires of flesh will overcome us. We will not be able to focus our thoughts on higher things. Yes, it is our minds taking us into the realms of reason to seek beyond emotion and the animalistic urges we have. Our minds realize the passing nature of these satisfactions. Thus, the mind also understands how limited we are, and this too is a good thing. The mind will either seek primacy or succumb to the passing degrees of time. A renewal allows the mind to continue in its rightful place. Reason is to lead us into contentment because the mind knows our limitations in what we can accomplish. The mind is aware of the infinite amount of knowledge to obtain, beyond the passing nature of emotions and desires of the body. Contentment is where we find unity and peace. Contentment comes from knowing and being secure in our place. The only place we can be truly secure is within a covenant with the unchanging God because God is eternal and immutable. It is God who renews our mind, which allows us to be led into contentment for both the passions of the Spirit and the pleasures of the flesh. Let me be clear: we should always be growing in Christ, allowing for a sense of urgency. However, the major sense should be peace and unity. With peace and unity, growth will occur. However, contentment is what keeps any part of our soul from hijacking control. The spirit worships as the body is present when the mind is renewed.

Balance between our trinity seeks complete agreement without compromise. A unifying goal will allow sacrifice without compromise because all the parties wish to reach the same end. This is how it is with God. The Trinity all seek the same thing, and thus sacrifice is done willfully. Think of Jesus in the Garden of Gethsemane. His prayers were for strength to remain unified. He was willing to make the sacrifice. That was why he came to Earth as man, after all. Yet, because Christ was both man and God, we can see this struggle to sacrifice himself, and we can learn two things. First, unity can be achieved. Second, it will be stressful. Christ in perfect unity, as God, sought to accomplish the goal of the Trinity. Yet as the man, we see the tendency and desire for singular self-preservation. We, too, have this desire.

The desire for self-preservation is not wrong, but it can be misappropriated. The mind and body may seek immortality and the spirit one last inspiration. There is a correct channeling of this, though it does require a unity of the three to attain. Do not you want to be in your early twenties and athletic and beautiful always? Do not we all want to make an intellectual contribution standing the test of time? Do not we want to inspire generations? It is in my heart for all three. Yet I feel constrained. I cannot complete all of these. I know my body will fade. My scientific contributions, if any, will be forgotten. My inspiration will lose its edge in the sea of time. When I reflect on this, I come to the same conclusion as King Solomon. "Eat, drink and be merry for tomorrow we die." The primacy of these desires misdirects us from caring for the whole. There is little unity in each of these pursuits, and the pursuits will often necessitate compromise. The compromise will leave us unfulfilled, as it did King Solomon.

By reaching unity, we attain this lasting peace and fulfillment of the self. The self can often be determined within relationships. Our relationship with God helps to define us and our strengths and weaknesses, and ultimately it leads to us playing a greater role as we become unified. But we need the divine to reach this unity to be fulfilled. Christ is the way to reach this unity. With Christ, our disparate pieces can be united for a lasting goal. He satisfies each piece. He remembers the mind, renews the body and brings worthy worship to the spirit. In this unity Christ calls us to something. He asks for something in return.

HOLY SELFISHNESS

What God ultimately calls us to is selfishness. He wants us to live our lives to our full potential. By reaching a full life, God is brought great glory. In our full potential, we worship Him fully and succeed in creating legacies as deep and old as the mountains themselves. This selfishness is not the selfishness we know. The selfishness we know is in fact not soul-serving. Living for ourselves only brings hurt, pain, emptiness and loneliness, just as it did for Dr. Jekyll, who sought to banish Mr. Hyde. Dr. Jekyll only increased his pain by attempting to remove part of his own soul.

We do not serve our souls very well by being selfish in the traditional sense. A greater potential awaits us. This potential can only be reached by serving God. His book, the Bible, details who He is and how to serve Him. By serving Him we reach full potential and thus truly serve our souls.

You may rightly ask why traditional selfishness is not soul-serving. There are a few points I would bring to the discussion. First, our selfishness is often not based on the best interest of our whole soul. It is often based on only the needs of one or two of the pieces of our soul. We know this is true. Reflect upon the times you behaved selfishly. Do they seem happy times to you? Do you remember them as fulfilling? When I think about those times, I remember how lonely I felt. I remember how I felt like I had wasted time. It felt like I messed up. This is not to make you and me feel like we are failures. It is to demonstrate the loneliness and pain common to all. We numb ourselves to both because we are unaware of a better way, but there is a better way.

There is a method to selfishness, however. The Bible calls us to find our self in God. God is constantly telling us we are important. We have meaning. We have purpose. He wants us to achieve our full potential. Through human means you can meet all the needs except one: the need for God. This is why God came down to us as Jesus the Christ. He wanted to fulfill the need for us. He wants you to reach your full potential.

Let me give you a couple of examples. We begin with Moses because he is touted as the humblest man. This is a very distinct title. Moses might have the most reason for pride. The Jews rightly exalt his faith. He led them from the thralls of Egypt. He led them back to the Promised Land. He trained his successor, who succeeded in reclaiming the Promised Land.

He had been trained for leadership eating at the table of Pharaoh. Yet, this man was able to remain humble. Why? You can sense that he reached his heights through someone else. God gave him the education, the skills, the direction and the support. Moses' full potential was to lead a nation. Yet, he could have remained comfortable in Egypt. Would he have become Pharaoh, perhaps? He could have made the political maneuvers to take the Kingdom and set the Israelites free. But he didn't. He found himself in God instead. The potential glory attained by him for bringing Egypt to their knees became glory for the Lord. As Pharaoh, would we remember Moses name? Maybe, as the man who lacked any ability to lead because he let his slave force walk away. He would have been remembered as a fool, and for leading a different nation. He is the author of a people's faith.

Let me also tell you about myself. Every day is a battle. Every day I must choose the Lord – over and over and over again, for I am an addict. I am addicted to escapism. I could read a good book for days and my wife would not be able to connect with me. I escape in video games. I love their stories. Many are truly an art. I escape into binge watching TV. I escape into things that have no meaning in the long run. Of course, I justify the educational value of books and movies and TV and video games, which have a potential high value. I justify it by thinking about how I am learning new things and being put in a great variety of situations, the amount of which is not attainable in a single lifetime. Yet, I leave work undone. My wife feels lonely. My friends feel uncared for. And I do not know the difference. You see, escapism is a tricky thing. If you do it well, you can fool yourself into not knowing the difference. Video games and books and TV allow to you to feel like you're making meaningful progress. You are not. I am not. I am running from my real purpose. For what reason I cannot tell you. Perhaps it is my lack of success. Perhaps I am scared of failure. Perhaps God opposes me due to my pride. I would like to think it is a bit of each of these, but the real truth is God is holding me in place. He has given me so much. Unlike Moses before me, I claim my cleverness. I shout my triumphs. The world revolves around me. I am the most important. But the truth is, I am not the center of the universe. This is deadly selfishness. You are not the center, either, even though I may think you deserve such an accolade. Neither of us are the center of the universe. God is. Like Moses, we must accept this truth to be the best we can. We need God to be the center so we do not have to be.

GOD DRIVES UNITY IN THE SOUL

This is a good thing for you and me. If you and I are not the center, then it is not all on us. We do not need to meet every need that comes our way. God will meet it. All we have to do is be humble enough to ask him. If you have need, God will meet it. Submission is the way to lead. As Christ points out, "whoever loses his life for my sake shall gain it." By finding our self in God, then we can reach our full potential and be completely satisfied, just like Moses.

Speaking of satisfaction, how many of you have ever felt complete satisfaction? I mean that deep-down-in-your-soul satisfaction – the satisfaction you get when you are congratulated for a job well done – the satisfaction you get because what you did or were a part of really mattered. You were a part of making a real difference. Do we not all seek want fulfillment? Who sets out in life to be a mediocre employee with a mediocre family and a mediocre income? No one does. Now some people achieve mediocrity in one area to achieve something greater in another. Perhaps you wish to provide for your family and excel in giving your children more than you had. Thus, you achieve mediocrity in the workforce in order to spend more time molding and shaping and growing your children and family. So, the satisfaction of seeing and understanding a happy family is what you work for. This is a good thing, but is it a Godly thing? You see, we like to make compromises. Making compromises is an important skill for many relationships, but sometimes we are just thinking small with God. What can we do with God? We can do anything, but it is not about ruling everyone else and receiving everything we have ever wanted. It is about doing His will. To understand this, you should meet Job.

Job was the man who had everything. He had a great family. He had incredible wealth. He actively sacrificed to God more than was required. Job 1:3 says this, "so that this man was the greatest of all the people of the east." The "east" here refers to all people east of Egypt. Ponder the greatness of his accomplishment. This guy is like Steve Jobs without all of the negative, or perhaps like Bill Gates and Warren Buffett as they would like to be viewed with their charity. Yet, when calamity comes upon Job, he does not praise God but extols his own deed, wishing to stand before the judgment of God. He calls the Lord to account for his actions. The Lord answers and Job understands his arrogance and pride and what they have wrought. He understands his separation from God, and he repents. He seeks the Lord again and the Lord blesses him. The moral of the story is that greatness achieved by our own design and pride is nothing. It is as useless as saving the world thousands of times in a videogame. Our greatness comes not from within but from without. Our greatness comes from God, so we must unite with Him.

We must unite with God in our soul through the Holy Spirit because it is the only way to unify our soul permanently. It is because our heart, which is the glue and center of our soul, will not be oriented correctly. The heart is the location of God's throne in our soul. While the whole soul may be the temple, the heart is the throne room. It is where the mercy seat is. The Holy Spirit continually reorients our soul toward Christ who is in our heart. This is how we achieve greatness and lasting satisfaction.

WHERE I MEET THE FALLEN

Jesus came to give us life to the full. To live life to the full, I need to realize my full potential and deepest desires. Sometimes, this is hard to understand what fullness means for oneself. We are too close to the situation to see it. Combining all our interests, abilities and passions into our life is an unenviable task with so many things vying for our attention. This is why my generation is so quick to not just change jobs but careers. We get into something we are good at, interested in or love but not all three at the same time. Our full potential lies at the intersection of all three. So, we learn to meet ourselves by doing and failing over and over again because nobody helps us understand the unified aspects along the way. But, somebody has been helping us, we just have not listened or been given the tools to listen.

God has been gently nudging us in the direction we need to go all along. Christians say, "God is calling them." The metaphor is apt because all we need to do to get His help is answer the phone. Answering the phone allows God to have a greater influence in an individual's life. God helps me meet me. He displays the deep passions of my spirit, the intellectual integrity of my mind and the pull of my body to connect with this world.

I write to entertain this call. I write poetry to probe the depths of my spirit as a telescope would reach into the expanse of space. I write blog posts to connect with the world in its present state, already outmoded tomorrow. I write books to stretch my mind, grappling with formerly impossible questions.

This is who I am. This is the fallen person I meet. Someone who has sprinted in a variety of directions just trying to be the best he can be, for his family, the world, God and himself. Frederick Buechner said it this way, "The place God calls you to is the place where your deep gladness and the world's deep hunger meet." I write because I find deep gladness and I am hoping to meet and fill some of the deep hunger. I hope you can meet yourself and, with God's help, have life to the full.

CHAPTER 9

UNIFICATION WITH NATURE

We have a responsibility to nature. When Adam named the many creatures of our planet, he understood them. He understood how each species had its own part to play. He named them according to this purpose. If each species has a special place of importance in its environment, then adding or removing anything to the environment would have an effect, or cost. Then what is our purpose beyond this naming? Our purpose is to determine the value of this cost. Why is it our job? It is our job because the creator gave us this purpose in Genesis 1:26 "... And let them have dominion over the fish of the sea and over the birds of the heavens and over the livestock and over all the earth and over every creeping thing that creeps on the earth." Dominion implies the social contract of ruling. Ruling effectively is counting the cost of any project – the cost not to just the ruler, but to what he rules or dominates. In the first part of this book, I argued about our failure to shoulder this responsibility. In this part, I want us to understand better the responsibility, so we can be unified and peaceful with nature. Our unity with nature revolves around us recognizing, understanding and respecting the cost our actions have on nature.

RECOGNIZING THE COST

Noblesse Oblige is a French phrase from the 1800s that literally means: nobility obligates. The idea attempts to communicate how nobility extends beyond entitlements (such as land or wealth) and requires the person who holds those entitlements to fulfill social responsibilities. In a general sense, wealth, power and prestige come with responsibilities to those who do not have wealth, power or prestige. Imagine, I were a wealthy person with a house much larger than my family could fill. *Noblesse Oblige* would dictate the need to hire a gardener, maid or both and perhaps even allow them to live (with their families) on the premises. It would not matter whether I needed a maid or gardener, only that I had means to employ them. By doing so, I ensure they are well fed and their children cared for. This allows my family to understand what it is like to not have wealth, and their families to have wealth to aspire to. You see, my wealth is not simply for me to hoard. It is there to raise the status of all those around me, men and women of equal power or those of less. The phrase, "a rising tide raises all boats." comes to mind. While *Noblesse Oblige* is typically applied in economic or social settings of the interaction between the rich and poor, we can apply it to how we interact with nature. As the dominant being in the relationship, it applies well to the recognition of where man and nature ought to meet.

Applying *Noblesse Oblige* to nature may not appear to have economical or societal impacts outside of how men treat other in the wake of a natural disaster. Consider this, though. Our entire economy depends on our ability to obtain increased yields from nature. For example, how does the cost of corn affect the price of smartphones. Corn is a base product. It is used in many foods as filler. Ground beef, for example, could contain up to 20% corn. So, an increase in the cost of corn increases the cost of meat. Even corn not consumed raw by humans or as filler gets fed to cattle, pigs, and other livestock. If livestock feed is more expensive, then all animal products become more expensive – from milk to manure. Milk in particular is used in baking processes, like bagels, donuts, muffins and cakes. Maybe you use milk in your coffee, too. Then, because the corn price is up, the milk price is up, and therefore coffee and bagel prices are up. The increase in price is known as a "cost of living" increase. If the cost of living rises, then salaries will rise to account for this – even the salaries of a smartphone manufacturer or designer. With the increase in salary, the cost of a smartphone must increase to compensate. In this manner we can see how the cost of corn (a product yielded by nature) affects the cost of a manmade good like the smartphone. In this manner we can see how our relationship with nature is very economical.

Beyond this notion of economics, there is a sociological impact as relates to *Noblesse Oblige*. If we are the stronger and more powerful member in this relationship, able to shape nature to fit our needs, then we ought to care for it as though we are the more noble in the relationship. Yet, we do not treat nature as though we are the more noble. We abuse or are apathetic or are too much in love with the created. We do not recognize the cost this has. There are two ways we fail to recognize the cost of our disunity with nature. The first realization is the failure to account for the personal cost of disunity with nature. The second is we fail to recognize the community cost.

The personal cost of disunity with nature plays out every day. Weeds grow in our gardens, birds poop on us, and the more complex idea about working to eat. In the book of Genesis, God curses us to have to work the ground. We now have to get down and pull weeds. Before, we did not have to work the ground – no weed pulling! We could no longer ask the birds to roost here or there. Farmers exist, and they labor in the ground to grow crops. Because of farmers, I can write this book. We have to work to eat. The earth no longer just opens up to us. It costs us time, blood, sweat and tears just to get what was once given freely. The cost of this is incalculable in pure economics. Even more so is the cost to our soul. Have you ever looked at your home and known you could do more and have more? So, we work harder to have more. We work harder and harder to the neglect of more important things, like other people, our families, our self and even our God – until the work is all we have. The sad thing is, we were not even designed to work as we do, just scraping by. God had us unified with nature, allowing a relationship to provide for our physical needs, but we wanted more. How do we get more? We refuse to care about the cost of nature even though inflation is ever present.

Beyond the cost to me personally, there is a cost borne by the community. The term "community" here is defined in the ecological sense.

In its simplest form, it refers to groups of organisms in a specific place or time. The cost then is not only associated with simply humans, but rather a group of organisms. We cause animals and plants to become extinct. These animals and plants have important roles in this ecosystem, and we can ruin the ecosystem by removing the animal or plant. Extinction has a cost. It may seem small at the time, but my grandchildren may never see a cheetah or a rhino. A plant species dying out may cause a bug species to die out, and so on until the whole system is affected. It is impossible to predict what the cost will be for the removal of any species. A bug may have the cure to a disease we have yet to encounter. The rhino may inspire an interesting architectural design or an engineering feat. The disappearance of the coral reefs will have devastating effects. Because of our irresponsibility with the costs of our disunity with nature, personally and communally, we cause more widespread problems.

The point of this is to find unity and ultimately peace with nature, we cannot just be abusive, apathetic or zealous. We have to recognize how our actions carry weight not just among other men, but in nature as well. Nature carries so much of our costs, and we do not care for it as we should. Ultimately this is our dominion. Nature will not have to pay the ultimate costs visited upon it. It is those to whom nature is subject. If the personal or communal cost is not enough for us to strive toward unity with nature, perhaps the accounting coming from God for how we used his creation will be enough to drive us at least to attempt unity with nature.

UNDERSTANDING THE COST

Romans 8:22 says, "We know that the whole creation has been groaning, as in the pains of childbirth right up to the present time." When Paul says, "whole creation," the term "nature" is what you should be thinking of for our context. Yet, how does this verse pertain to the cost of our actions? The cost is in the groaning. Groaning, however, does not sound that bad, though. After all, my wife groans every time I make a bad pun. This groaning, however, is equated with the most painful experience we can imagine – childbirth. Nature has been in this painful process for thousands of years. The cost of our actions keeps all of creation in the greatest pain we can imagine, and there is no epidural. This verse gives us an understanding of the cost when we are not unified with nature. Nature groans because of our irresponsibility and will continue to groan until unity has been achieved again.

The cost of our actions does not just end with birth pains for an entity with which we do not connect. The cost was also carried by Christ. Christ came to save us, but he also gave us clues into our relationship with nature. He calmed the storm (Matthew 8:23-27). He wilts the fig tree (Mark 11:12-14, 20-25). Jesus feeds the 5,000 and walks on water. He demonstrates dominion over the "natural order." We have forgotten how to rule nature because we are not united with it. Christ has given us a chance to see and understand what we might be capable of through the power of the Holy Spirit, a restoration of what we should be. Christ paid with His life for these examples and the mending of all the separations. He understood neither us nor nature were living up to our potential, and it was a result of the curse against us. He came to die for us (in part) so we could reach unity with nature. Why? The answer is tied to how all of creation (including us), living up to its fullest potential, brings glory to God, and nature has a purpose in allowing us to relate to God.

Imagine you are the God of the universe and you want to create beings to which you can relate. Since God is a ruler and has dominion over everything, a good being to relate to is one who is also a ruler with dominion. God gives us a dominion, so we have something to talk about with Him and something by which to relate to Him. He lets our dominion train and refine us, so we have something intelligent to say over dinner with God. For a relationship to work, there must be shared values and experiences. The purpose of nature is to give us these values and experiences, so we can better relate to God. God does not want an ethereal or fake relationship. The point of Christ's coming is to ensure our ability to have a relationship with God. Without Christ, we cannot tap fully into any unity, even nature. Therefore, having a relationship with God is more difficult because it is harder to relate to a just ruler if we are not just rulers ourselves. So, the cost of mistreating nature is not just carried in the groaning of nature, but it is costly to our relationship with God. If it is costly to our relationship with God, then are we in danger of hell, the place where God's presence is not found. We should see it as a choice – care for nature, rule justly and grow closer to God, or abuse our power, rule tyrannically and move away from God. That is the price we pay for our disunity with nature.

RESPECTING THE COST

Understanding the cost, even though it is personal and communal, is not enough. Our actions will ultimately show unity and lead to peace with nature. Respect comes from the idea of the privilege to rule nature. If it is our privilege to rule nature, then we will do what is best for it. The actions of just rule are found through Jesus. He understood the relationship nature was meant to serve. Out of this relationship, He was able to act by bending the rules of nature without abusing or harming it in the process. By this He was able to bring glory to God.

I live near the Smoky Mountains. There is great beauty in the fog and strength and age of the mountains. They are impressive in a very different way from the Rocky Mountains or the Alps. They are not as tall or as snowy or as formidable. Yet, they still bring God great glory in their uniqueness. They fill a role no other mountain range can fill, simply because of its location, among other things. There is also a park, a conservation effort, surrounding the Smoky Mountains – called the Great Smoky Mountains National Park. The Park Service is there to protect the mountains from harmful effects brought about by humans or nature. It is there to allow the mountains to be. The Park Service cuts roads and trails and maintains, so more people can enjoy their beauty. Next to this park, towns have grown up – the towns use the mountains to generate tourism and industry. The people are able to make a livelihood from the location of the mountains, and in turn they must protect the mountains. The people gain glory from protecting the mountains. God gains glory because the mountains are still there, and He can reveal His power and majesty through them. This is an example of the respect we can have for nature without abusing it or overvaluing it.

The Smoky Mountains also provide examples of potential disunity. First, abusing the Smoky Mountains in order to generate more tourism in the short term would ultimately destroy their beauty. Tourism would then decline. Second, if the mountains were overvalued, no one would be allowed to go near them to experience their majesty. They would become overgrown and unwieldy, ultimately leading to the destruction of the beauty of the mountains which we sought to protect. Overgrowth would also be detrimental to the human efforts of getting through and around the mountains.

Nature is present to serve us, and we are here to protect it. *Noblesse Oblige* drives us to view nature not as a foreign thing, but as something living in our house and needed to run our lives. We decide how we use nature. If we do well, then nature will reward us as God rewards us. If we do poorly, then nature will disown us, like a mother who abandons her child after too much suffering.

WHERE I MEET NATURE

I always learned to appreciate nature from my parents. We were involved in Boy Scouts and camping for as long as I remember. We also worked our land as a family. Now when I say land I mean the normal suburban quarter or half an acre, nothing grandiose. However, we mowed, weeded, planted, and cared for our tiny plot of land every week. When you care for your space like my parents did and you pass it along (although my brother and I frequently resisted), you teach respect. You teach how to care for the ground, the plants, the trees and the water. I learned how to work the ground, so it could be beneficial. Without an actual garden, we treated our whole plot as our own garden.

Now, I have begun to do the same with my son. One of his favorite things to do each week is yardwork day. We mow, weed eat and (his favorite) use the blower to clean off the driveway and spread out any grass clumps left behind. We trim our bushes and plant flowers for Mom too. But, I do not let this just passively sink in. I talk to him about how we have to take care of the land. I talk about why we trim the grass or cut back the weeds. I talk to him about cultivating the land. He is still a little young to get it all, but it does sink in. He does not mash or crush flower. He respects them and likes to show them off. He cleans up if sees trash lying around. My son has subtly learned to care for the environment where he lives.

It is important for all of us to learn this quality. Perhaps, you start a rooftop garden in New York City. Perhaps, you catch one less fish today so there are more tomorrow. Perhaps, it is just landscaping your suburban home to maximize the healthiness of the earth. Regardless of how you do it, you are giving back to the earth. You are caring for your sons and daughters for generations to come because this is our home, and we should treat it with respect.

CHAPTER 10

UNIFICATION WITH MAN

This is a book about relationships. So far, we have explored building our relationships with God, ourselves and nature. Finally, we wrap up with the relationships between humans. Early in this book we looked at how choosing the knowledge of good and evil divided our perspectives on how to act. Good and evil became a personal perspective. Prior to this good and evil were external. We never needed to know good and evil. We only needed to act in accordance with God's will. It was a simple will – act as kings and queens of the Earth. Treat each other, nature, ourselves, and God with the respect due to them. We did not choose to follow God's will. Instead, we sought to forge our own path. That path has led to conflicting opinions about everything and has made the truth difficult to find. The knowledge of good and evil soured our relationships because we did not agree with one another all the time. Even Cain and Abel demonstrated how good and evil are a perspective.

Now, we have Christ. He calls us back to a singular purpose and a singular view. He gives us a simple command structure. Love God then love others. The idea of the Kingdom of Heaven is not a complicated one. It is, however, a difficult one to live out. It can be simple with an ethereal God, ourselves, or a planet we are meant to rule. It is another thing to work with people we do not like. Still, we are called to not like everyone but to love them. This love is how we are to be known as followers of Jesus, as his disciples.

Discipleship is what Jesus left us. He did not author a book. He left no writings. He left us a group of imperfect people who were told one thing: love each other as I have loved you (John 13:34-35). Through this love they were meant to spread Jesus to the whole world. You see, the Bible is not the message of Christ, love is the message. Our relationships are the message of Christ when we love one another. We are meant to love each other moving us away from separation anxiety and toward a unified peace. We are meant to be in relationship with our fellow person, the world, our self and God. Relationships are the measure of peaceful unity we have with one another.

As Christians, we can look at two relationships to help us determine our peace and unity. First, we can view our relationships with those outside the Church. Are we loving them the way Jesus did? Do we come to their houses and eat with them and care for them? Do we break down barriers for the lowest of society to become the highest? Is this occurring on both and individual level and a Church community level?

Second, we can look at our relationships within the Church. Are we acting as a holy nation, a royal priesthood? Are we connecting with those inside the Church? Are we being a family? How are we interacting with other Church communities? Does it look like we are a family to those outside the Church? Are we kind and gracious with other sects, or are we threatened by them?

With these two relationships in mind, we can look through Jesus to see how we are doing. We can look at an issue, like abortion, and begin to understand how to act. Then we can look at our own lives. Are we acting as the disciples of Jesus? Finally, we will look at the communities of churches.

UNIFICATION WITH THOSE OUTSIDE THE CHURCH

Earlier in the book, I brought up abortion and called it murder. I still hold that to be true, but the growing number of abortions, the ease with which they are performed, and cultural acceptance of abortion are not the fault of the women on whom these procedures were performed. Let me say it this way: the women who had abortions did not dictate the culture surrounding them. The people in power did. Men, the protectors of women, dictated the culture around us today.

The 1973 U.S. Supreme Court Case Roe v. Wade is about protecting women.[15] It is about letting them get a safer medical procedure. It is not about killing unborn children. Roe v. Wade stepped in to protect women in the most minimal way possible. I imagine the Supreme Court Justices making the decision hoped the Church would heed their natural call and duty to protect these women. After all, is not pure religion this: visiting the fatherless, the widow, and the orphan?[16] Christ himself said whoever does this for the least of these, you have done for me.[17] Getting an abortion is a low point. It puts you near the least of these. What has the Church done to heed the call?

Nothing.

We, the Church, have not heeded the call. We are the problem here. It is not for the Republicans, the Democrats or anyone else to decide how to protect these women better. It is for the Church to freely offer sanctuary to all women regardless of their choices. It is our role to save these babies and these women. It is our role to give them refuge. It is our fault that so many have died either in unclean procedures or because of clean procedures. It is my fault for ignoring the anxiety in society.

The Church's mistreatment of women is not limited to the issue of abortion. The #MeToo movement spawned a #ChurchToo movement. The pervasive harassment and disrespect shown to women is appalling. The Church ought to be a place of safety and refuge, and we have made it a den of thieves and robbers. At least the government is willing to stand up and protect women. The Church sure has not been willing. We are supposed to be more loving than the world, but it was the world who has exposed our faults.

We do not love like Jesus when we mistreat someone. We do not love like Jesus when we harass those outside of the Church. We love like Jesus when we reach out to and give of ourselves to make their lives better. Harassment makes no one's life better. Shaming a young woman because she fell in love with a stupid boy does not make her life better. Shaming a woman because she was abused does not demonstrate the love of Christ.

Taking the downtrodden, the shamed, and the abused into our homes, our buildings and our facilities is the first step. We then clothe them, walk with them, talk to them, get to know them, and finally they feel love. We re-train them to feel like they are worth being loved again because they are worth it to God. Our mistreatment has trained us, both men and women, to act as though people are not worth being loved. Men are viewed as an oaf. Women are viewed as sex toys. These are our brothers and sisters. We will be co-heirs with them one day. A sex toy does not befit the title of your sister. Stupid oaf does not befit the title of your brother. We are meant to encourage one another while it is today.

How do you stop the things of this world that are against the teachings of Christ? You love them. Love gives people value. You take in the teenager who was molested and you teach her that she is valuable. You demonstrate her worth to you. You give her value because she is a person. If she chooses to have an abortion, you might strongly recommend another option, but what is the other option? You might have to continue to care for her and her new child. You might have to walk with her through the heartbreak that adoption sometimes leaves people with. You might have to walk with her through the travesty of an abortion. At the end of the day though, you walking with her gives her worth.

Being told you are worth something changes everything for the least of these. It changes your life and it changes the lives of your children after you. Is there a better time and place to step into someone's life and have a lasting impact than a woman who just needs someone to help her out? We, Church, have missed the mark. We have sinned in this endeavor to prevent sin. We have shamed, and disrespected ourselves and others. We must be better. We must protect our women and children. We must die for them as Christ died for us and the Church.

How does Christ treat us for our sin? He dies so that we might live through it. We, his disciples, should do the same.

VULNERABILITY

If we are called to Christ, then we are called to vulnerability. Christ radically calls us to leave our safety and security and find it in a new place, Jesus who is God. Earlier I wrote about vulnerability being the path through the separation anxiety. We have to expose ourselves but we are not without protection or hope when we do so. Jesus is our protection. He is our solidarity. God came down to suckle, poop, sleep, and die with us. Jon Sobrino said it this way, "God does not display his omnipotence by conquering the negative reality from the outside. Instead he does so by immersing himself wholly within it and thereby displaying the power of love."[18] His ultimate expression of love demonstrates the vulnerability God was willing to go to. God was willing to be vulnerable to death on a cross.

Can we take in women to save them and children? Can we protect the poor, the weak and the destitute? Can we love the LGBTQ+ neighbor? If you believe them sinners, do you think Jesus would have been at church or eating with them? I think Jesus would have reached the communities the Church hates because he lived it in his age by spurning the Pharisees and eating with tax collectors. Then he died for both the Church and those the Church would come to hate.

Vulnerability rather than power is the way for us to move beyond our insecurities. Vulnerability is the way to show love because when we are vulnerable we immerse ourselves in the negative reality in the same way Christ does. How do we immerse ourselves in reality? There is a prayer written by Nehemiah revealing how the path of vulnerability is lined with humility. Nehemiah's prayer inspires my actions with both the community and within the Church.

Nehemiah is part of the exiled Israelites in Babylon. He was too young to be a part of the exile and becomes of leader of the return to the region of Judea. He is the cupbearer to the King, an important ranking official. Here is the piece of the prayer that always sticks out to me.

> confessing the sins of the people of Israel, which we have sinned against you. Even I and my father's house have sinned. We have acted very corruptly against you and have not kept the commandments, the statutes, and the rules that you commanded your servant Moses. Nehemiah 1:6-7

Nehemiah is confessing the sins the community has committed. Notice, he is taking personal responsibility for the actions of his people. He was not even a part of the crimes, and his family was most likely a group of the most righteous among the Israelites. Rather than placing himself a part from the sins of Israel, he owns them. Nehemiah goes before God in this prayer with radical vulnerability. He exposes himself, his family, and his community for the crimes they have committed. Vulnerability invites

God to be active in our lives. Nehemiah's vulnerability, ultimately, allowed the people to rebuild Jerusalem.

Church, we have sinned against God and against our fellow man. We have not kept with God's desires for our lives. My family and I are a part of this sin. Beyond my nucleus my Church family is in this sin. I appeal to you Church. Return to a vulnerability and therefore a solidarity with the people we have mistreated. Love the woman who has been abused. Love the LGBTQ+ person who lives down the street from you. Love our wives and daughters who have been abused so much so that a Twitter movement must shake us from our slumber. Become the servants we were always meant to be.

Now, this is not going to happen overnight. Sin exposed and vulnerability embraced can cause quite a shock to the system. Begin small and work great. Perhaps the simplest thing we can do, Church, is have the best marriages. Our marriages are already supposed to be where we are most vulnerable. It is a small and comfortable place compared to radical vulnerability with strangers. If you cannot be vulnerable with your partner, then perhaps you have been mistreating them or mistreated by them. However, there is no better place to begin a vulnerable relationship than marriage because it changes your perspective and behavior toward those outside the Church.

MARRIAGE

Wives, submit to your own husbands, as to the Lord. For the husband is the head of the wife even as Christ is the head of the church, his body, and is himself its Savior. Now as the church submits to Christ, so also wives should submit in everything to their husbands.

Husbands, love your wives, as Christ loved the church and gave himself up for her, that he might sanctify her, having cleansed her by the washing of water with the word, so that he might present the church to himself in splendor, without spot or wrinkle or any such thing, that she might be holy and without blemish. In the same way husbands

should love their wives as their own bodies. He who loves
his wife loves himself. For no one ever hated his own flesh,
but nourishes and cherishes it, just as Christ does the
church, because we are members of his body.

Ephesians 5:22-30

In the New Testament, Jesus and the Church are often visualized as a marriage. Even as a married man, I find this relationship difficult to understand. So, we are going to have to break this down into some chunks before rebuilding it. By understanding our relationship with Christ in the context of marriage, we can begin to uncover how we can be unified with those inside the church. If we are all a family, it is helpful to understand mom and dad's relationship.

Remember, man and woman in the garden were equal in all things except time spent on the Earth. Adam simply had a time (days, hours, centuries, millennia?) on the Earth before Eve. Thus, she would have naturally looked to Adam for some guidance, as anyone would look to an elder or mentor for advice. In God's eyes, I believe they were equal but different. They had different roles to play. After the fall, these roles were well-defined. The man was to have authority or rule. The woman was to be his helper, submitting to his authority. Let's discuss these two roles.

AUTHORITY

Let everyone be subject to the governing authorities for
there is no authority except that which God has established.
The authority that exist have been established by God."

Romans 13:1

Men, what have we wrought with our authority? We have seen nations rise and fall, magic realized in scientific discovery, art almost beyond comprehension, and so much more. So why do we languish in laziness? Let's be real, I am lazy, and if you are reading this book, then you are probably at least a little lazy too. Do you know what laziness with authority has created? Things like slavery, starvation, genocide, persecution, and oppression come out of our laziness, which is born from our pride. We were lazy in our authority over Eve, and we have not grown from then until Abraham until now.[19] Let us not be this way anymore! We are depriving ourselves of the greatest adventures and struggles and life because we are lazy. Let us rise into the sacrificial authority of the Lord Jesus Christ!

What is this authority? Where does it come from, and how can we execute it properly? This authority came to us upon creation (Genesis 1:28) and was further accounted for in the Fall of Man. In Genesis 3:16, God says to Eve, "… your desire will be for your husband and he will rule over you." Our authority is from God and its purpose is to lead our family. Have we done a good job?

If you have been to a worship service lately, you will notice a common occurrence of more women than men in the seats. Almost worse is many of the men there will appear completely disinterested. Why? Because we are lazy. We are not interested in putting forth the effort to create or maintain a relationship with God because it gives us little immediate or easily visible benefits. A relationship with God simply bores us, no? This is no surprise, as most of us cannot even be bothered to maintain a relationship with anyone beyond our significant others. Yet, our wives seem so invested in this God. They care so much. Why not let them lead in this relationship? She leads in almost all the others. So, what? We have the authority to get it done, but we just let our wives carry this heavy load because we do not care to engage. Do not get me wrong, ladies. Women are incredible administrators, surgeons, communicators, artists, musicians, singers, philosophers, and governors. Women obviously care more than most of us, men. Why not just let you do everything? Then, we men can just sit in front of the TV and be a security force. Maybe, we can do some heavy lifting. Do you see our laziness has thankfully allowed women a freedom they have long been denied, but have left us men without purpose? I believe God gave us authority so we would always have purpose. Women have the vitality and drive to accomplish, but it is our role to be the leaders.

Thus, our authority comes from God in Genesis chapter 3. But this authority is not a power meant to abuse. It is power meant to sacrifice. On average, are we not bigger and stronger and more physically powerful than the women around us? Yes, just as Christ was more powerful than those around him. We are imbued with the same power – not to subjugate but to sacrifice as Christ did. Thus, we can look to his example for authority and how to execute it.

CHRISTLY AUTHORITY

Looking at Christ and His use of authority will teach us how to execute our own authority. He first used His authority to maintain a relationship with the provider of that authority, God. Men, if you are tired of watching TV or being badgered by your wife, and you want more out of life, it begins with God.[20]

A relationship with God is no easy thing, however. It requires a growing commitment. You have to do things like read your Bible, pray, participate in Bible discussions, lead family devotions, pray with your wife, listen to your wife, teach your children about God, lead a small group, give money to the Church, submit to Church leadership, confess sins, repent of those sins, lead, rule, have fun, mourn with, pray with.... the list goes on and on, and it will eventually take more and more of your time. If you are doing the whole relationship-with-God thing correctly, then you will spend more and more time doing Godly things.

A relationship with God is not just a laundry list of to-dos. He does not make a "Honey-Do" list. The things I listed above may not all be a part of your experience. Many of them do come out of having a real relationship with God. The relationship will change your life from the humdrum American lifestyle into something special, but it requires a ton of effort and a whole lot less laziness. Christ first used his ultimate authority to commune with God. See Luke 5:15-16:

> Yet the news about him spread all the more, so that crowds of people came to hear him and to be healed of their sicknesses._But Jesus often withdrew to lonely places and prayed.

After communing with God, Christ lived with purpose. Christ spent every moment of his ministry purposefully. He poured himself out to twelve men who could take his message to the world. Jesus probably always went to bed tired, but that good kind of satisfying tired. He conversed with the Pharisees, healed the lame, drove out demons, and still found time to teach twelve men what it all meant. He did all of this ultimately to die. He purposefully strode onward toward his death, not for his own sake, but for ours.

The conclusion is our authority is meant to be selflessly spent. My authority is not there to grow massive amounts of wealth so I can own more stuff. My authority is meant to save and sacrifice for people. Maybe I will have massive amounts of wealth, and my purpose could be to generate a massive amount of wealth, but it is not so I can live in luxury. Remember *noblesse oblige* from the last chapter. Wealth is present to give to the needy and poor. Wealth would be mine to spend as fast as I could make it, not on the latest tech gadget (as I would prefer), but to spend it on hospitals, food, shelter, and education for members of my society who would never have the chance otherwise. Maybe a story will give you some perspective on what I mean here.

In Luke 16:19-31, there is a rich man and a beggar named Lazarus. The rich man lives in luxury every day. Lazarus hopes for the crumbs of the rich man's table. Eventually, they both die. The rich man goes to torment and Lazarus goes to paradise where Abraham is. Abraham's response to the rich man as to why they are separated is this: "Son, remember that in your lifetime you received your good things, while Lazarus received bad things: but now he is comforted and you are in agony." How often did this rich man pass Lazarus and do nothing to aid his fellow man? Probably almost every day, and yet he did not even give him the crumbs off his table.

You see, the rich man sacrificed nothing to help someone in need, and he was put into torment for it. Lazarus, meanwhile, did not succumb to the temptation of stealing, trickery, or evil and was comforted in the end. The purpose of me using this story is to direct our attention to how each man used his authority. Lazarus did not use his authority to steal or harm the rich man as we might feel is our right to do. The rich man did not use his authority to help the man sitting at the gate to his mansion. God gave both a measure of authority, and it was Lazarus who proved trustworthy and sacrificial. He sacrificed his own well-being to not steal or harm the rich man. He chose to live in squalor. The rich man sacrificed nothing, not even the bread crumbs.

From this story, God wishes us to use our authority to sacrifice for others. To see ultimate proof, we need look no further than the cross. In the garden, Jesus wished three times that He would not have to die, but in the end, He endured it for us and the Father's will. He sacrificed Himself so we could have a relationship with God. In the end, a life lived to the full is one sacrificially spent. You get to use all the God-given power and authority. You and I must execute our authority by submitting to God and sacrificing for others, just as Jesus did. By submitting to God, we lead others to Him.

SUBMISSION

Submission is such a dirty word today. It has no honor or place in our society. Submission, like humility, is for those who cannot be strong. It is only for the weak. I think this is silly. Only the truly strong may be humble, and the greatest have the highest need to submit. Otherwise, it is only an act forced upon someone – a false act that may give the one forcing it a momentary feeling of conquest or victory. But true submission or humility is freely given.

While men may have the authority in the marital relationship, I wonder how often it occurs to us the vital role the women play. I am a smart man, but in so many ways I fall short of my wife. I have often heard the joke about just saying sorry to your wife because the wife is correct in almost any argument. Why is this a joke? It is because the joke is seated in truth. It is good that our wives are wise and intelligent. If my wife were not correct most of the time, would I heed her advice? Probably not! In this way she begins to fulfill her role as the helper Eve was meant to be. Eve was the crowning achievement of creation, the glory of God and man alike. God made her as a helper, however. Dominion was given to Adam, not Eve. Here is the crux – while Adam was given dominion, it was Eve's to assist, not to control or to dominate. If she is choosing not to control or to dominate, then she must be submitting, in humility. Women, this is a true submission, freely given. Women, we men need you, but you would not be needed if you were inferior beings. You are called to submit, which is different than men called to be the authority. In turn, men are meant to sacrifice for you in the same way Christ sacrificed for us. Did not Jesus die for the glory of His Church? In the same way men, you need to sacrifice yourself for the glory of your wife. Ladies should you not submit to someone willing to die for you? It is difficult, of course! We men do not often make it easy. The call from God remains the same though.

What if you choose not to submit? I have spoken about why you should submit, but what are the consequences should you choose not to? Well, if the man is the authority, then he will be accountable for his charge – you. Your insubordination may cost your husband because he is called to lay down everything for you. Think of it this way. If Christ died for us while we were in sin, your husband is called to follow his example. He, too, must lay down his life for you, even in your sin. How much more joyful would his sacrifice be if you were to be his helper along the way?

SUBMITTING TO CHRIST

> "This is a profound mystery – but I am talking about Christ and the church."
>
> Ephesians 5:32

If Christ is the authority as the husband is, then the Church's role is submission. We cannot supplant Christ with another person. Christ still lives. We simply have to follow his lead. That raises the question of how do we follow Christ? While the answer is simple the act is difficult to execute.

The difficult part of following Christ seems to be our intoxication with his authority. We seek to use his authority as our own. Most often, the Bible is used to provide Christ's power to its wielder. We like to hold someone's salvation hostage for behavioral modification simply because we are better studied in the texts. The Bible, however, gives no such authority to men. If Christ did not consider equality with God a thing to be grasped, then we too must consider equality with Christ a thing not to be grasped.[21]

Like Christ, the Holy Spirit resides within us. The Holy Spirit is not to be used to claim equality with Christ, who is our author. The Holy Spirit helps us discern what it is to follow Christ. We are not alone even with the Holy Spirit. The Church community helps us discern the presence and authority of Christ without claiming any authority in the process.

The New Testaments writers were masters at this practice of humility. They comment on the presence of Jesus without claiming any glory themselves.[22] The early Christian writers guided us in tangible opportunities to submit to Christ by writing the Bible.

The Holy Spirit and the Church community marked by the Bible will educate and increase our faith in Christ similar to how we tell wives to submit to her husband.[23] Growing in faith decreases the separation between our fellow person because we seek to aid each other in humble submission to Christ. We are no longer deciding, but it is Christ who decides.

WHERE I MEET HUMANITY

This is how my wife and I live out our marriage in our lives today. I am the Chief Operating Officer (COO) of our family. The decisions about where and how and what the family is doing run through me. It is my job to ensure our family is prospering. As COO, I must continually check in on the family and adjust our course for the needs displayed. I wake up in the middle of the night for kids. When my wife is exhausted from long hours at work, I take the kids for a weekend morning out so she can rest. It means when I need rest, I have to ask for it from my wife, and sometimes I am just out of luck. As COO, I lay down my life for my family in the same vein as Christ. I do not take jobs outside the goals established for our family.

My wife is the Chief Financial Officer (CFO). All my operational decisions need to be run by her to make sure we have the available resources to complete the project.[24] In this way, she makes sure that we are successful as a family. It also forces me to check in with my wife before I do something I will regret.

You might be wondering who is the Chief Executive Officer (CEO) of our family. God is. My wife and I operate on the same business level in our family. I might outrank her when we go head to head, but God always has the final say. He is the support we need to accomplish the goals and tasks set before us. She can always ask God for more resources. I can always ask Him his thoughts on how to operate in a certain area. We have our roles, but neither of us is alone on top. We work together as partners underneath the real leader of our family, God. As we break our own traditions, this mindset has saved us time and time again from problems that could be potentially marriage and family destroying. To me, this is how God meant for the church to be modeled. Men are meant to take some charge underneath Jesus, but we do not outrank the women. They are just as deserving of their executive level status. In the end though the Church submits to Jesus as my wife and I submit to God.

UNIFICATION WITH OTHERS

In the beginning of this book, I argued that separation with our fellow man is about a skewing of a singular purpose. Christ unites us under a single purpose. He gave us an example of how to manage relationships with the example of his outreach to the disenfranchised and with his marriage of the Church. He removed the good or evil question. With Christ as our authority figure, there is no need for us to determine what is good or evil. There is only Christ. When you read through the Old Testament, you can get the sense God is constantly attempting to woo the Hebrews. As he gives rules and laws, he constantly notes how things will go well for the people if they only obey. You can get this sense best in the accounts of the kings. There are "good" kings who do evil in the sight of the Lord, and in the end, it does not go well for them. "Good" in this sense means they grow the wealth of the kingdom and they rule well, but they do not follow the Law.

In the New Testament, there is no good or evil. There is only Christ. "Take joy, my brothers, in the sufferings that you endure for the sake of Christ." Suffering is almost always bad or evil. Yet, the apostle Paul will tell us it is good if we do it for Christ, thus removing whether a ruler, king, magistrate, or judge is good or evil. There is only Christ and his singular purpose, which is to bring heaven to earth. We now wait together eagerly for the second coming. Yet, there is much work to do. He does not just give us a long-term goal that is difficult to see. He gives us unifying work to do in the meantime. We are to love one another as our own self and through this make disciples of all nations. This unification removes the desire to judge. We are all simply using our gifts and talents to reach the end goal which is to spread the privilege of the love of Christ.

UNIFICATION OF THE CHURCH

With Christ as a singular authority and providing a unifying vision – a vision which we share with Jews – you should be able to find a group of people with singular purpose driven to the pursuit of glorifying God with honor being shared among all as their gift allows. Why, then, are there so many Christian sects? A non-believer can simply look at our disorganization or even animosity towards other Christian sects and find the hole in the logic surrounding the "love one another way." Why, then, can we not unite? What is holding us back? A simple answer might be pride, but I think it is so much more. I believe men throughout history truly wanted to follow Christ. They were just not willing to be humble before other men. Let me give you some context.

UNITY AMONG BELIEVERS

In Christianity you will find disagreement over the tiniest of details. We disagree over so many things – from whether we should have Bibles on every pew to whether we should even have pews to whether we should have music in Church to whether we are appropriately evangelizing or raising our family right. At the end of the day, there is no silence. We yell, scream, and clamor for *our* way. We, as a group, are not silent before Christ when it comes to maintaining orderly worship. I have been a part of these discussions, and I am ashamed to admit my participation in the brawl. Brothers, Sisters, can we not find our humility before Christ and each other? Put aside your differences. Be quiet! Learn to listen to the Spirit, for He receives his orders from Christ. Make every effort for Unity! How much stronger could we be if we only united our many different limbs into a singular body of Christ!?

I will show you how to begin.

To my Roman Catholic brothers and sisters, the Pope and all those priests under him, I apologize. I have not made every effort to unify with you. In fact, I have worked against you and have thus doubly sinned. You stood before the rest of the faith even began. Teach me your love for Christ. Please forgive my sin against you.

To my Eastern Orthodox brothers and sisters, I have never attempted unity with you. What knowledge of Christ you must have! May you one day share with me and all my brothers your deep understanding of the Gospel. I have sinned in my lack of effort. Please forgive me.

To my Jewish brothers and sisters, you must know most of all. Your blood heritage gives you an ancient ancestry. I apologize for all of Christianity. We treated you with exceptional harshness. You have born it with the grace of God. Your wisdom reaches deeper than my greatest dreams. I, we have sinned against you for the longest of all. Let me begin to make restitution by acknowledging the strength of your faith. For without your commitment through slavery, exile, occupation, genocide, I might not have a Messiah. I am nothing without you.

To the variety of Protestants brothers and sisters, I have thought ill against you. I have thought you silly or stupid for splintering further and further. There are many reasons for which a wedge may be driven. You often have legitimate grounds to split. I urge you most of all to reunite. As you reunite, I ask you not to throw away all your learnings and all of your traditions. In our uniqueness, God has built the Bride of Christ. I ask you to submit humbly underneath the authority which is Christ. I apologize for working against you as well. Forgive my many sins because they are as numerous as the number of different sects.

Through honoring the strengths of each group, we gain a unity. The Catholics with the numbers and history have a tradition but lack the vigor of the young Protestants to evolve continually. The Orthodoxies bring in a necessary deep wisdom that cannot be ignored if we are to succeed in our mission before Christ. All are needed. We must find unity in Christianity. For there are terrible storms to weather. All abilities will be needed and used.

EPILOGUE

As someone who loves the violin and classical music in general, it has been a great privilege of mine to enjoy many recitals and concerts. After one such concert, I was speaking with one of the members of the orchestra, complimenting them on the music. He told me it was not his best work and there were many mistakes made, especially in the beginning. He complained that the conductor had asked more out of the orchestra than they were prepared to give. Instead of saying no one noticed, I told him the truth. Yes, there were many mistakes, but the music played on and the concert was great because they overcame the adversity of those mistakes instead of letting them continue to build. The concert ended up being a success because of the mistakes. It forced the musicians into playing with one another instead of playing their pieces individually.

Not believing my words of encouragement, I told him this story. There was once a great composer/conductor and two great violinists. The composer looking to get the most out of these violinists arranged an unbelievably demanding piece for them. Neither the first nor second chair could master the piece. So, he sent them home with a practice piece even more difficult than the one assigned. He asked them to record themselves as they practiced, and he wanted them to bring a recording of perfectly played music to him by the end of the week, Friday morning. The first chair violinist immediately went home and began working on the piece. He was determined to keep his place as first chair and prove himself to the composer. He worked for hours and hours but could not get the piece done correctly. After making notes, seeking advice, recording and more recording, bleeding fingers and hours of frustration, it was late Thursday night, and he chose his best recording to give to the composer, though it was certainly riddled with mistakes.

The second chair violinist also immediately began work on the piece. As he played, instead of becoming more frustrated, he began to hear the music in the piece. After days of loving work, he decided to ask his mom to listen to his work. As he played each note tenderly and lovingly, with mistakes to be sure, his mother added a tear to her eyes. When he finished, she hugged him and thanked him profusely for playing for her. He turned in the recording to the composer. "Which do you think the composer chose as the better violinist," I asked my friend? "The second chair, of course," he answered. Then I asked him why because both players had made mistakes in their recordings. He answered, "because the second chair understood that he was not just playing notes on a page, but a musical piece of art. He came to understand his part of something larger." This is what happened tonight, I explained to my friend. Tonight, while imperfect, the whole concert came together because you all played music instead of notes on a page.

Do you see the metaphor I have laid before you? God is the composer. We can play His music beautifully but filled with mistakes. To do so, we need to appreciate the music and the privilege of playing it. We do not play by ourselves, though we play with a concert hall. We get to play as a violinist with base drummer, the flutist and the trumpeter. Because we play with them, we make music. I tone down the trumpeter, but he powers me along in the music. We both need each other to play this music the Almighty God has composed for us to play. It is in our need for one another and the composer that we find it our privilege to love the music, the musicians, and the composer.

ENDNOTES

1   Twenge, Jean M., PhD. "The Age of Anxiety? Birth Cohort Change in Anxiety and Neuroticism, 1952-1993,." *Journal of Personality and Social Psychology* 79, no. 6 (December 2000).

2   *Oxford Dictionaries, by Jacob Pannell* "separation," accessed October 22, 2018, http://www.oxforddictionaries.com/definition/english/separation.

3   Bible quotes are from the ESV unless otherwise noted

4   *Oxford Dictionaries, by Jacob Pannell* "anxiety," accessed October 22, 2018, http://www.oxforddictionaries.com/definition/english/anxiety.

5   I acknowledge that God is without gender as both male and female are made in his image (Genesis 1:26). While certain aspects of God may take on masculine or feminine characteristics in general God is without gender. The English language, however, has no gender-neutral pronoun. While one may argue the "it" is gender neutral, it fails to capture the essence of a being on the scale of human or greater. To improve readability of the text, I use the English neuter, him or he for God. I attempted to capitalize throughout the text to increase clarity of whom I was referring.

6   Brown, Brené. "The Power of Vulnerability." Speech, TEDxHouston, June 2010, October 22, 2018.

7   Waldinger, Robert. "What Makes a Good Life? Lessons from the Longest Study on Happiness." Speech, TEDxBeacon Street, December 2015, October 22, 2018.

8   "Abortion Statistics: United States Data and Trends." National Right to Life Committee. Accessed October 22, 2018. http://www.nrlc.org/site/factsheets/.

9   1 Corinthians 11:7

10 Genesis 3-4:14

11 Job 38

12 I first learned of the concept in a sermon from Matt Chandler.

13 Nelson, Roger D. "Coherent Consciousness and Reduced Randomness: Correlations on September 11, 2001." *Journal of Scientific Exploration* 16, no. 4 (2002): 549-70. Accessed October 22, 2018. http://noosphere.princeton.edu/papers/jseNelson.pdf.

[14] Bonhoeffer, Dietrich, Reinhard Krauss, Charles C. West, and Clifford J. Green. *Ethics*. Minneapolis: Fortress Press, 2015.

[15] Roe v. Wade (January 22, 1973).

[16] James 1:27

[17] Matthew 25:40

[18] Sobrino, Jon. "The Historical Jesus and The Christ of Faith: The Tension Between Faith and Religion." *Cross-Currents*, 1977.

[19] Despite being the father of three of the world's largest faiths, Judaism, Christianity, and Islam, Abraham is not always so courageous. Twice, Abraham tells rulers his wife is his sister because He fears for his own life. Genesis 12:10-20 recounts the tale of Pharaoh and Abraham's relationship. Genesis 20:1-6 recounts the tale of Abimelech and Abraham's relationship. In both cases Abraham essentially sells his wife to the Harem of these rulers. That is some laziness and fear. We need to exercise care and protection, not sloth and greed, especially when it comes to our wives.

[20] A worthwhile book that explores a fulfilling masculine life is <u>Wild at Heart</u> by John Eldredge.

[21] Philippians 2:6

[22] Philippians 3:4-8

[23] Ephesians 5:21-32

[24] Luke 14:28-30

CPSIA information can be obtained
at www.ICGtesting.com
Printed in the USA
LVHW092128270219
609015LV00005B/21/P